Table of Contents

Preface
Welcome to the Equestrian Adventuresses Tribe!

Thank you for being a part of this wonderful adventure. Putting together a collection of stories from women who speak a variety of languages and have traveled far and wide on horseback hasn't been easy. We've featured women's amazing true stories throughout this series, including adventuresses from Poland, Belgium, Australia, the USA, the UK, New Zealand, Germany, and many others. Their inspiring stories have taken us to places such as Georgia, India, Mongolia, Italy, Canada, South Africa, Namibia, Romania, Greenland, Chile, Argentina, and Bhutan.

In no other equestrian book series has so many international readers and riders come together in one place and I am very excited to say that because of these stories' young girls in Yemen, India, and others can be taken to faraway places on horseback and be inspired and encouraged to follow their dreams.

Having spent more than a decade working with horses in male-dominated countries where women are not allowed to ride, this book series has been a dream come true for me. When I was a little girl, unable to afford horse riding lessons or a horse of my own, I would lose myself in books and stories of girls riding horses and having adventures. I told myself that one day I would be surrounded by horses and it was because of books like these that fueled my ambitions into one day turning into a reality.

These pages contain true stories. Many of the authors do not speak English as a first language. Although we did our best to edit the stories and translate their words, a few minor mistakes here and there are expected for a big project and undertaking such as this. But the stories are what counts and these women didn't hold back! They bravely take us to unexplored lands, trail blaze new paths, and journey across exotic destinations, all from atop a horse.

I hope you enjoy each and every one of their stories as much as I have and remember to share this book with as many of your friends and future adventuresses as possible! You never know which story might spark the hidden flame that enables someone's life to change forever. I hope these tales empower future girls and women around the globe to saddle up, head for the horizon, and see where they end up.

"My heart belongs to the arena but my soul belongs to the trail." - *Anonymous*

Yours Truly,
Krystal Kelly

Founder of Equestrian Adventuresses
www.EquestrianAdventuresses.com

The Quest for Panch Kaliyan in India

BY UTE TONIA PETERSKOVSKY

I was sitting in a tiny turboprop airplane descending towards Udaipur airport. It was September and everything was green. I had my nose glued to the window and took in the scenery with all my heart. India here I was!

After finishing my schooling in Germany, I had no wish yet to go to university and continue years of study. I wanted to see the world and get some experience and insights into different cultures and countries.

I had been lucky to find a job with a member of the royal family of Udaipur. A relative of the Raja of Udaipur had a stable full of horses and a liking of Germany, coming with the notion, that German girls were all excellent riders, well-disciplined and perfectly suitable to apply this discipline, to overseeing his stable of Marwari horses. What else could a young, crazy-for-horses-girl wish for?

My employer had sent a car to pick me up, an old-fashioned Ambassador, a white formerly luxurious limousine with deep seats, threatening to swallow up the unsuspecting passenger and a gearshift attached to the steering wheel. Ambassadors used to ply Indian roads for many decades until the liberalization of the Indian economy and the succeeding influx of modern, more economic cars made them obsolete.

We drove for about ten minutes on a bad road towards the city when a sudden torrent of rain made my driver pull over to the side as his car did not have any wipers on the windscreen. We patiently waited for the rainstorm to abate, together with a few cows and dogs who took shelter from the rain under the overhanging roofs of some dilapidated buildings on the roadside.

Once the torrent was over, we resumed our drive until we reached the horse farm, my new home for the next twelve months. My arrival had not gone unnoticed, and I was welcomed by a stern-looking man wearing a khaki uniform and a red beret cap.

He looked at me from top to bottom without a smile or any other facial expressions and waited for me to give him my particulars. I told him that I had applied for a job and had been accepted and gave my name and country. That seemed to satisfy, and he gave a curt nod, took my backpack, and prompted me to follow him.

We went down a little passage with an assortment of horse stalls on both sides. An evil-tempered black stallion was the first one to catch my eye. Later I learned that he was the famous Sultan, a respected and sought-after sire of many foals. I saw some horses roaming a spacious, dusty courtyard and some confined to stables. My heart raced and my spirit rose. We arrived at the main house which once in time might have been considered grand. Now it was run-down and rebuilt with many small and cheap additions, a room here, and a terrace there, all miss-matched and a bit tattered.

My room was on the ground-floor and roomy with a huge poster bed and some cane furniture. I closed the old-fashioned double door behind me and sank on the bed.

My new employer received me in the afternoon over a cup of tea. He was a remarkable man, tall yet bent with age. I judged him to be above 70 years, and with a frown on his face, yet gentle eyes, sparkling with humor.

He ordered two cups of Indian chai and sat down to talk to me about horses, the one great passion of his life.

Lifting his bushy eyebrows, he told me, "Settle in first and then slowly oversee the work of the horses; riding the older ones, training the younger ones, just as you feel right."

Then he asked me the question I had been dying to hear: "Do you want to go for a ride now?"

Of course, it was just the thing I wanted to do! He called a groom to make two horses ready and bring them. Two horses were produced, a bay thoroughbred gelding named Rustam and a beautiful black Marwari mare with four socks and a blaze called Radha. Radha was given to me, and I was in heaven. The mare was all-around lovely, responsive, and kind and I loved her the minute I put my eyes on her.

I had seen Marwari horses before, yet for those who have not, let me tell you about their unique feature, their ears. They are not straight like in other horse breeds but curled inwards at the tips. Often the tips of their ears meet, sometimes they overlap. Besides the odd shape, the ears are also incredibly flexible and turn 180 degrees. Now Radha had overlapping ears which fascinated me at once. She stood there waiting for me to mount and her ears were dancing, a moment focused on me, then focusing on something behind her. They turned like radar antennas, picking up each little sound or movement around her.

Riding her was a pleasure, Radha was responsive even though let loose, she sprang away in a powerful canter and would have increased speed if I had let her go. I returned to the farm in the last light of the day, dusty yet happy.

Soon I settled in a rhythm. Feeding in the morning was done by the grooms, then there came the grooming and if I wanted to work or ride any horses, I could just do as I pleased. Once the head groom, Ghomera, returned from his village, he took me out riding every day, showing me the riding routes in the surrounding countryside and making me try out different horses. I soon settled on some favorites. The gentle Radha, but also a beautiful bay mare called Rosy who was a favorite of my employer, and the jet-black, cheeky mare Sabrina who knew each short-cut home. She would turn abruptly from full-speed gallop in the direction of home when grasping that I did not know or pay attention.

I started working with the three-year-old colt Suraj, a stunning golden chestnut who had the same markings as his mother Radha, four white socks, and a large blaze on his forehead. I had but little experience with young horses, so Suraj became my student as well as my teacher. I was lucky that he was so patient and gentle for a three-year-old colt that I never had any problems with him.

I soon grew to like and treasure him like no other horse. His coat was a mix between red and gold and radiated when the sun shone upon it.

I taught him jumping, and we jumped every stone wall and fallen tree we came across.

As I grew more familiar with the terrain, I spent hours riding through the countryside, getting to know each path, hill, and valley. The landscape around Udaipur is hilly as the city is situated in the Aravalli Mountains, an ancient mountain range, now rugged and degraded to mere hills by wind and weather.

I made a friend in Jay, the nephew of my employer, who came to help at the farm now and then. He loved horses just as I did and came to be near them and ride them whenever he could. He did odd jobs for my employer which the old man could no longer do himself. And soon he also taught me Hindi, and we had many long and interesting conversations.

After some weeks had gone by, I decided to go to Jodhpur for a long weekend to see something of the country and get some fresh vistas. It was a 7-hour drive by bus over the Aravalli Mountains and in order to save money and time, I took the night bus. The days I spent in Jodhpur were interesting, packed with sightseeing, and also strenuous. I was happy to go back to my peaceful life with the horses.

When I returned to Udaipur, I discovered that Suraj, my project for the last weeks, had been sold. The transaction had taken place in my absence and had been conducted quickly as he had already been taken away. I was devastated as I had grown quite fond of him. My employer perceived my disappointment and tried to humor me, but failed. I had never known that he wanted to sell him, otherwise, I could have prepared myself.

I felt a deep void I had not known existed, even when there were still plenty of horses around me to ride and train.

The next day Jay came back and asked me about my Jodhpur trip. I answered him gloomily, so he probed and soon found out the reason for my depression. He tried to mock me and pointed out, that I would not have been able to take him home with me anyhow, so why was I so morose? He had a point there, but then such fancies are rarely reasonable.

Jay promised to find out who had bought him and take me there so that I could say a proper goodbye and see for myself, that he had found a good home and was happy.

He went in to talk to my employer while I went to tidy up the tack room, a Herculean task I had wanted to tackle for some time.

My head was covered in cobwebs and I had found and dislodged more than a few unwelcome occupants of the saddle room, in the form of spiders, mice, a nest of rats, and a small snake, when he returned triumphantly. He told me that Suraj had been sold to a horse trader called Kuldeep whose farm was situated at the other side of Udaipur and that I could go and meet him if I wanted.

There was no question of that and it was settled to go and meet him the next day.

I was able to bring a measure of order into the tack room before I went to bed that night. My last thought was of a golden-red horse before I sank into Morpheus' arms.

The next morning dawned bright and warm as usual and I was up early. At 10 o'clock, Jay came to take me to Kuldeep's farm. It was a half an hour drive as Kuldeep's farm was on the other side of Udaipur in the countryside. The farm was smaller, yet well-kept and a good number of horses were stabled there. Kuldeep himself was not in, but we were welcomed by a small, Indian woman who made us sit on a terrace in the shade and served us—as is the custom in India—a glass of water.

I looked around and saw several horses tied up at the side and eating their measure of hay. Some were colored horses, a bay and a grey, but no chestnut. In a field, there were two mares with foals. Behind a little farmhouse, I had seen some other horses, but it would be impolite to get up and look around without the owner being there.

At length, Kuldeep returned and came to where we were seated. He was a middle-aged man of dark complexion with a streak of gray in his hair. He greeted us friendly enough but with a bit of a skeptical eye. As it was custom in India, Jay started talking about the weather, the crops, and horses in general before he asked him about Suraj.

Kuldeep offered us chai, without hearing our polite refusal, and then answered in the affirmative, "Yes I have purchased a chestnut colt last week, but indeed, I have already sold him again." He looked almost apologetic.

"That was a quick sale then. Who purchased him?" Jay asked.

"I sold the horse to Salim Bhai. He came to visit and took a fancy to him, as he is of a good bloodline and a Panch Kaliyan."

"What is a Panch Kaliyan? I inquired, curious as I had heard the term before yet had no idea what it meant.

"A Panch Kaliyan is a horse with five white spots on the body," explained Jay. "Such horses are described in the ancient book of Shalihotra as highly auspicious! People pay a lot of money for horses with such markings."

"So, Suraj is valuable then!" I exclaimed. "I had no idea!" Kuldeep smiled and nodded. "It is not only the coloring people look at, but also the conformation and breeding. And of course, the whorls!"

"The whorls?" I asked incredulously. "Yes, there are favorable and unfavorable whorls." Kuldeep said and pointed to a nearby horse, "Look. This mare has one whorl on her forehead above the eyes. That is auspicious. If the whorl is below, people believe the horse to bring bad luck. A horse with two or more whorls on the forehead is considered a difficult horse."

Finishing our chai, we got up and thanked Kuldeep for his hospitality, and went on our way back into the city. We had missed Suraj, but Jay was not deterred that easily.

He proposed to go to see the wedding horses of Udaipur, the place we would find Salim Bhai, and possibly Suraj.

Udaipur's wedding horses could be mostly found in the Muslim quarter of the Old City as most of the jobs related to horses were performed by Muslims. Traditionally horses were owned mostly by landed gentry who needed them for administrating their estates and to ride into battle, but since medieval times, horses were brought to India from Central Asia and Arabia by Muslim traders.

When we entered the labyrinth of tiny streets and lanes near the mosque, Jay parked his motorbike and we proceeded on foot. It was a part of Udaipur, I had never been to. Like everywhere in the Old City, the houses had small shops on the ground floor and living quarters above. Each house was built wall to wall to the next one. Besides the shops, small doors and gates led to the inside of these houses.

Where would the horses be kept? I wondered. There were no fields, no open spaces for them. Yet I trusted Jay to find the right way and quietly went along. It was around noon. The day was hot and the sun stood in its zenith. Most of the streets were deserted, the people had retreated indoors.

We stopped at a small white house with a green door. Jay called out and a small, slightly aged man with grey hair and a hawk-like profile, emerged. I knew him from the farm; it was Jamal Bhai, the farrier who came once a month to shoe the riding horses. Jamal Bhai looked at us with an air of surprise but then ushered us into the house. We entered the small green door and went through a narrow passage, which opened into a large, courtyard. Here the family was sitting and having their lunch. Jamal Bhai's wife and daughter-in-law were making chapatis on a gas stove in the open-air kitchen which was situated under a tin roof shading a part of the courtyard. Three men were sitting cross-legged on a carpet on the terrace eating their food. Jamal Bhai invited us to sit down and join them. We took off our shoes and did as we were told. A girl came and gave me a plate with food and some warm chapatis—Indian bread—which smelled delicious.

We washed down our food with spiced buttermilk and when the men got up one by one and left us alone with Jamal Bhai, Jay approached the subject. As they spoke Hindi, I did not understand much, even though I had studied it a bit and learned a few words and sentences.

I got up and joined the ladies in the next room which was connected with the terrace by an open door. Besides the two women who had made the chapatis, there were three other ladies and around five children of different ages sitting in the room having their food. They had been clearly speaking about me as they burst into a volley of giggles when I entered. One of the women got up and invited me to sit with them. She spoke English and introduced me to the rest of the family. I spent a pleasant half an hour with them when Jay entered and beckoned me to follow. Jamal Bhai did not know about whether the horse was still there or not, but he had told him where Salim Bhai kept his horses, so we could go and see them.

We decided to come back in the late afternoon when it was cooler and people would be up and willing to receive us.

It was around five o'clock when we went back to the Old City. Unlike before, there were more people on the streets now going and coming and we had to proceed slowly. Salim Bhai's horses were kept in the heart of the Old City behind a red iron gate. On the way, we had passed a few horses, almost all white. "Wedding horses," explained Jay, "are usually white as that is deemed most auspicious. The groom rides a white or grey mare to his wedding venue and feels like a prince for one night!"

He saw my smile and continued, "Originally it was only a Rajput custom, but thanks to Bollywood, now everybody wants to do it! These horses are called Nukra, they have pink skin and a white coat from birth onward, unlike grey horses which are born colored but turn grey and finally white with each passing change of coat. Nukra horses are highly prized and used almost exclusively for weddings. It is a handsome income for their owners."

The wedding season had started but not yet reached its climax. We saw some horses being readied but most of them stood tied to some hook or ring in a street corner eating some roughage out of feed bags or troughs. Why would people keep their horses here I asked myself? Jay seemed to guess my question and told me, "A horse is a valuable possession! People like to keep them close to make sure they are well taken care of and nothing happens to them!"

Even though I felt sorry for the horses being tied up on concrete streets and corners, I saw that almost all were well taken care of. Their coats were shiny, their feet and fetlocks painted with Henna, a strong antiseptic which prevents thrush and other diseases, and many had food in front of them.

Finally, we arrived at Salim Bhai's place. Jay knocked at the gate and a small boy of maybe ten years opened, shyly peeping out. After an exchange of words, he bid us to come in and scrambled off, presumably to find Salim Bhai.

We entered a spacious courtyard where about ten horses were tied up side by side. They were attached in front by ropes around their neck and behind on one foot.

"Like this, they can lie down if they like but they cannot turn and kick each other." Jay pointed out.

Indeed, all horses were well-behaved—there was no bitching or kicking despite the crowded conditions. Alone a little white foal was allowed a measure of freedom and relief from restraint. She scampered about playfully and went from horse to horse to eat here and there a bit from different mangers. I wondered how her mom had brought her into the world in this confined space. I let my gaze sweep over the horses but I only saw white ones. No chestnut horse was here. But then, it was all mares and no colt or stallion.

The arrival of a large, stately man, clad in a white Salwar Kameez, an Indian dress of a loose-fitting trouser and a long tunic, interrupted my train of thought.

Salim Bhai invited us cordially to join him for a cup of tea inside his house. He listened carefully when Jay explained to him our quest. He shook his head and answered back. The whole exchange was in Hindi of course so I had to wait until Jay deemed it proper to translate for me. Salim Bhai had indeed purchased the horse but had sent him to his brother in his native village, who would train him in dancing before he could be sold for a handsome profit, he explained. Here in Udaipur he kept only his wedding horses, no horses for training or trading as he simply did not have a lot of space. Well, that was obvious, but I was getting more and more frustrated. It seemed that we were chasing a ghost. Through how many hands had my poor Suraj gone in the past few days I wondered.

Before leaving, Salim Bhai offered to show me his favorite mare, Nagina. We stood at the entrance of his house and he told the boy a few words. The boy opened the ropes of the mare at the end of the courtyard and Salim Bhai gently called out to her from where he kept standing. The mare lifted and turned her beautiful head and gazed at her master. She then came towards him in measured steps. In front of him, she nickered and he took out a lump of molasses which he fed to her. Despite my sincere dislike of the way these horses were being kept, I could not help noticing the profound love the man had for his horse and the affection the mare felt for him. They had a deep connection with each other, something I could not quite grasp and which I never had encountered before. It made me more determined to find Suraj and bring him back to me.

Jay and I spoke little on our return journey to the farm. When he delivered me back, I asked him, "When do you think is a good time to go to the village and meet Suraj?"

He looked at me in surprise.

"Why do you want to go?" he asked me. "It is a journey of thirty, forty kilometers over dusty country roads! The horse is gone and you should come to terms with it!"

With that speech, he left me to go back to his home in the city.

That night I lay awake on my bed thinking about the situation and about Suraj. Why did I so much want to go and see him? What would or could come out of such a visit? What was I thinking? Maybe Jay was right, I should put him out of my mind.

Jay did not come back for three days. Perhaps he was afraid that I would be angry with him or would argue with him to go.

I went about my work quietly and tried to put Suraj out of my mind. Yet when I closed my eyes, I saw him. I dreamed of riding him and I dreamed that he turned his head towards me and called out to me.

When Jay came back to the farm, I had made a decision. I would go to the village and find Suraj. I had to go, maybe just to see that he was well taken care of, and I would go alone if necessary.

Jay seemed to read my decision from my eyes. He looked at me, sighed, and told me that we could rent a taxi and go early the following morning.

Unfortunately, a guest arrived at the farm for a week of riding lessons that very afternoon, so we had to postpone the trip for some time. My attendance was needed to provide lessons and take the guest out on rides.

I was happy to finally be of some use to my employer, but I was also frustrated that it prevented me from going to the village.

I kept my impatience under guard and tried to enjoy my work. The guest finally left after one week and then my employer had other work for me, he wanted to present one of his yearlings to his relative, the Raja of Udaipur. Apparently, the Raja had come over one day I had been out on a ride and expressed his interest in the colt.

And as my employer could not very well sell the horse to him, he had to gift it to him. The logic was lost on me, but my employer asked me to ride out with three of his boys to present the colt to the Maharaja at his stud farm.

The black colt called Ganesh had been born on a very auspicious day, the birthday of the elephant-headed Hindu God, Ganesha. He was very ostensibly a son of Sultan, being of the same color, having the same marking and the same regal manner as his sire. His mother was my favorite Rosy, so he was a beautiful horse, having inherited his mother's good looks.

We set out two days later on a day deemed auspicious enough to deliver a royal gift. There was four of us on horseback and one boy on foot leading Ganesh who was gleaming with his mane and tail freshly washed and combed out.

We all wore khaki breeches and red berets and looked rather a smug company setting out early to avoid the heat of the midday.

The ride to the stud farm was not long, maybe five kilometers, but it was mostly through villages slowly being swallowed up by the city. The roads were paved, but we had to ride leisurely anyway as the boy with Ganesh was walking. Thus, we arrived in the late morning hours at the stud farm. We were awaited by the head groom, the compounder and a few attendants. I was disappointed as I had secretly hoped to meet the Raja himself.

The stud farm was a pretty place. We entered through a big gate and passed through a huge area of grazing pasture for the horses. As the rains had not been long ago, the whole place was green and lush. A herd of thoroughbred mares with foals had looked at us from a little distance away and our horses whinnied and called out to them.

The stables were built of grey stone with white-colored fences and gates. The grooms all wore proper red uniforms and everything looked bright, clean, and tidy. I felt like being in a military camp as the grooms saluted us when we passed the gate and entered the courtyard. We dismounted and stood by our horses. Ghomera presented the colt and the head groom welcomed him with a small religious ceremony. He held a round silverplate or thali with a little oil lamp and various smaller items I could not quite make out and circled it three times in front of Ganesh's nose. Then he presented the horse with a large piece of molasses, which was munched away contentedly. Subsequently, they lead him into his new stable. The head groom thanked us and we were offered chai and snacks before we returned home.

It took me another two days to finally organize a car and tie-up with Jay to go and look for Suraj. Jay was not at all very happy at the prospect of driving forty kilometers to some obscure village to look for a horse. But he did not want to let me go on my own either. So, at six o'clock on a Tuesday morning, we were finally off.

The drive was long and tiring. Neither Jay nor the driver had been to this village before, so we took a few wrong turns and did not arrive before almost noon. Once arrived, Jay got down from the car but made me stay inside to wait for him. He went to a group of men and talked to them with a lot of animation. It felt like an eternity until he came back and pointed the driver down a dusty country lane presumably towards the farm of Salim Bhai's brother.

The driver grumbled, it was hot and he wanted to return as soon as possible, but ultimately, he turned the car and headed down the lane. We drove another two kilometers before we came to a little path made of caked mud leading towards a grove of trees and what seemed to be a riverbed. After fifty meters, we came to a gate. Jay jumped out and opened it. We passed it and came to a farmyard with a two-story house and some stables next to it.

I quickly got down from the car before Jay could tell me to stay inside once more. I was feeling hot, sweaty, and impatient. I just could not wait another minute. A man in white clothes with a skull cap came out of the house to meet us. He welcomed us and invited us yet again, for a cup of chai. We sat down on cane chairs on his terrace while his wife, head and face covered up with the end of her sari, came out to serve us some water.

Jay had an animated discussion with him for what seemed like hours. I looked around and tried to spot some horses, but I could not see the stable from the terrace and there were none in the garden or the adjacent fields.

Finally, Jay turned towards me and told me that Suraj had been here but that he had been sold to the Thakur of Khulwa, a village around 100 km from here, and that they had taken him away around five days ago.

I groaned, again we were too late. The ghost we were chasing had yet again disappeared!

Jay continued talking for a little while, then got up and took his leave with folded hands. I imitated him and we went back to the car. The driver had put down his seat and was deep asleep.

I stopped Jay and looked at him. "We have the car, let us go to Khulwa. Now we have come so far, we can also continue!" I said.

He just looked at me, shook his head, and muttered something which suspiciously sounded like "madwoman!" And, he was probably right, it was sheer madness, but he woke the driver and gave him new directions. The driver argued with him for a while, then gave in and we resumed the drive.

Khulwa was close to Ajmer and it took us the rest of the day to reach there. Jay knew the Thakur of Khulwas family, the widow was an aunt of his father and her two sons had studied in Udaipur along with Jay and his brother, so we drove straight to Khulwa Fort, the residence of the family. I could easily see the former grandeur of the fortress, even though it had clearly seen better days. The driver dropped us on the porch and Jay told him to await further instructions. We entered the main gate which was open and looked around. We stood in a huge courtyard surrounded by high walls on all sides. The main house seemed to be on the left where a number of lighted windows shone in the imminent dusk. An old, gnarled looking man in a white Dhoti and turban approached us and questioned Jay. He replied and the man bade us wait in a little room with some chairs. While we awaited his return, Jay quickly told me about the family connection and the history of the fort.

"Khulwa Fort was once the seat of a powerful noble family but after Independence, the family had lost all means of income and was reduced to poverty, like so many others. Only in recent years, the sons have found good jobs and returned a measure of the family's old prosperity.

I know them from school, the older son lives here in Khulwa with his mother. He is called Anand and he likes horses. He keeps a few on a farm nearby. The younger son, Ajay, was in the same class as me. He lives and works in Mumbai."

Presently the old man returned and we were escorted into the drawing-room of the castle. Like many old buildings in India, it had a regal air about it, yet was a bit run-down with old furniture, crumbling plaster, and faded curtains.

Soon afterward, a young man burst into the room. He gave Jay a handshake and then a hug and was very obviously glad to see him. The two of them spent some time talking animatedly in Hindi, until he finally turned, perceived me, and immediately apologized in perfect English that he had so far ignored me. He bid me welcome to his humble abode and invited us for dinner which was about to be served.

Jay told him about our quest and his friend, who introduced himself to me as Anand, immediately told us that Suraj was currently in Pushkar, as there was the famous Pushkar Fair and horse market going on at the moment. I had heard about the Pushkar Fair, it was the largest camel and horse market in Asia and also a religious gathering. I had wanted to go and see it, but so far, my search for Suraj had prevented me, so it looked as if I was about to experience it anyway now.

Anand had entered Suraj in the horse show which was to take place tomorrow and he hoped that he would gain a prize and he could sell him for a handsome profit.

Over dinner, he asked me all about my connection with this horse and he had only words of praise for his manners and behavior. I glowed with pride.

As it was already very late when dinner was finally over, Anand told us to stay overnight at the fort. He did not accept no for an answer so we relented. Jay would sleep with Anand in his room and I was assigned the guest room, a most stately chamber with a huge four-poster bed and rich wall hangings. The bathroom was basic though, but I was so tired from the long drive, that I did not care much but fell into bed, deep asleep within seconds.

The next morning a knock at my door woke me up. I needed a minute to rouse and orientate myself. Where was I? Finally, everything came back and I jumped out of the huge bed. I got dressed and went to the dining room, or rather, tried to find the way back. I ended up in the kitchen where a woman was busy preparing tea. She took the tray and led me to a terrace where Anand and Jay were already sitting. We had chai together and then decided to set out to Pushkar. The horse show would start at eleven o'clock. We drove with Anand in his comfortable Sumo, having told our driver to stay at Khulwa and rest for the day.

The drive from Khulwa to Pushkar was about one hour. During the drive, Anand told me many interesting facts about the Pushkar Fair, how the horse and camel market dated back to medieval times and was a major place for the trading of horses coming down from Afghanistan.

The closer we came to Pushkar, the more excited I became, finally I would see Suraj again and get the chance to experience the famous Pushkar Mela.

We reached Pushkar by mid-morning. It was still time until the horse show would be held in the large Mela ground. We drove to the sand dunes around Pushkar where the horses were tethered in large numbers. I looked in awe at what seemed to be thousands of horses. Finally, Anand stopped his car in front of a large tent. He had brought two of his horses, Suraj, and a mare which would also be taking part in the horse show that day. Both the horses were stabled—or rather, tented—together with the horses of a friend and horse trader from Ajmer. I got down from the car and immediately I saw a chestnut head with a broad blaze. My heart skipped a beat and I crossed the distance in a few big steps. Suraj seemed genuinely happy to see me and more so, the piece of molasses from my pocket. He looked good, his coat was shining and he was well-groomed and fed. I rested my head against his neck and breathed in the sweet horse scent. The ghost was real after all! He turned his head to me and slobbered molasses all over my sleeve.

Anand introduced us to his friend Kutub Bhai who owned the tent and the other six horses standing there. I looked around. Anand's piebald mare Lakshmi stood in one corner with two boys grooming her. The other horses were mostly mares and one more colt standing next to Suraj. The colt was a nondescript bay colored horse with a large star on his forehead, probably a two-year-old.

We had a cup of chai brewed over a small fireplace behind the tent. Chai and food were made by the wife of one of the grooms who had accompanied the small troupe.

In the large tent, there were five Indian beds called charpoi, bedframes wrapped with strips of cloth. People sat on them, ate their food on them, and slept when they were tired. A very versatile piece of furniture indeed!

After the chai, the boys took Suraj, the piebald mare, and another black mare belonging to Kutub Bhai and led them to the show ring. We also decided to make a move, so that we still could get some good seats.

The Mela ground was a large oval ground with a podium running around half of it, covered by a sky-blue metal roof. The podium had no chairs, just benches of concrete, but there was shade and we got a good view over the show ring.

The first horse show was the milk-teeth filly class. Fillies below four years of age could participate. All were pretty, but I did not really pay attention as the colts were already in sight and I noticed Suraj.

Next came the mare class and here Anand proudly took over the reins of Lakshmi. Unfortunately, the winners were not announced immediately so it was quite boring as there was not a lot of action. The horses were lined up and inspected in walking and standing.

Finally, it was time for the colts. Suraj was one of eight colts being judged. He looked good, a bit small next to a huge black colt, but handsome enough.

The colt ring seemed to last only a short time, then it was the stallions' turn. I did not have the patience to stay and as Anand also was keen on getting back to Kutub Bhai, we left the Mela ground and headed back to the tent together with the horses.

The winners and runners-up were announced only later in the day and Anand was happy that Lakshmi got third in the mares' class while Suraj did not win a prize which disappointed me a lot. He was too small and too narrow in chest, Jay decided. I objected but maybe it was a blessing in disguise as Anand sighed that now there would be little interest in him.

"I want to buy him!" I told them, but both laughed and did not take me seriously.

Anand asked me if I cared for a ride over the fair later in the afternoon. I did and so we set out once the heat of the day had waned. The ride was magical. Anand rode his mare, Jay one of Kutub Bhai's horses, a big-boned bay mare with a blaze and a white hindfoot, and I was seated on my beloved Suraj.

The dust mingled with the sunset, giving a warm golden light and the world smelled of cow dung fires. While the trading had been slow during the day, it became brisk now with buyers trying out horses and sellers showing off their animals. We crossed over to the camels which looked at us curiously. Suraj was not quite sure if he liked these large, ungainly animals or not, but he bravely followed the other two horses through the lines of camels.

At last, we left the market behind and reached the sand dunes beyond Pushkar. This place was known as sunset point and a few camel carts had ferried some tourists there to enjoy the vista. This did not disturb us and we urged our horses into a gallop over the dunes, racing each other, as our horses' hooves hardly touched the sand underneath. Galloping over the soft underground felt like flying as there was hardly a sound except for the whistling of the wind in our ears.

The night we spent at the Pushkar Fair, sleeping comfortably in the tents close to the horses. I stayed in a little separate tent together with the two groom's wives and their three small children. For the kids, it was very exciting to sleep in one room with me but I fell asleep even before my head touched the pillow.

The next morning dawned and I woke from the sounds of the animals, the clattering of cooking vessels, and the smell of tea. I got up quickly and went into the main tent. Anand, Kutub Bhai, and Jay were sitting on a cot, drinking chai. I was handed another cup and Jay told me that we would return back to Udaipur tomorrow morning. My employer had told him there was some work in Pushkar.

It suited me well, as it gave me time to explore the market and town. I was out and about as soon as I finished my chai, wandering around the fair, and looking at the scene. Horse owners took their animals to the water troughs for drinking. Others exercised them, making use of the early hour when the lanes of the market were not yet crowded.

The nights were cold, just as the days were hot, so most horses were wrapped in rugs, made out of rough jute sacks, sewn together. Now as the morning progressed, the rugs were taken off and the horses brushed and massaged.

A whole herd of camels was driven towards the dunes, mayhap sold and heading towards their new home. Small food stalls were busy preparing tea and breakfast for those traders who did not bring their own food with them. Life floated along its path just the same as in all of these hundreds of years the Pushkar Fair had been taken place and I would venture to guess, that it would continue to do so for another hundred years or more.

I sat down in the Mela ground watching some riders racing their horses in the typical reval, a fourth gait some Marwari horses have. The hooves of the horses flew over the deep sand of the area and the total lack of the clip-clopping sound made it appear almost surreal.

A trainer took a mare and did various steps of horse dance with her. Her colorful bridle was gleaming in the morning sun and she was sporting a bit of sweat as the first hint of the heat of the day was creeping in the fresh morning air.

Later when I got hungry, I returned to the camp, entering silently to find Anand, Kutub Bhai, and some men I did not recognize in deep conversation. I sat down on a cot at the back of the tent and watched the proceedings. The conversation stretched over multiple cups of chai, lunch, and into the afternoon.

The group went to see some horses, checked teeth, hooves, and whorls, and then returned to the cots to continue the discussion. They were obviously interested in Anand's mare Lakshmi. I could not understand more than the occasional word, yet it was fascinating watching the men so intently going about the business of buying a horse.

Once, Anand got up, shook his head, and made a move to leave the tent. Quickly one of the men jumped up and persuaded him with many gestures and words to stay.

Finally, after many hours, the mood suddenly changed. The men had reached an agreement and there were many congratulations, joy, and noisiness. Some bundles of rupees were pushed towards Anand and one of the men untied Lakshmi and sent her away with a boy who apparently had been waiting outside.

Kutub Bhai also left and Anand remained behind. I went to congratulate him and he asked me to sit down with him. He was in a pensive mood.

"You know, Lakshmi was born at my farm and I am really sorry to see her go," he said.

"I understand how it is to grow attached to an animal like you are with Suraj. Still, I sold Lakshmi. I got a lot of money for her which will pay for my expenses and enable me to cover some of my mares with a good stallion and have more foals next year. And I know she is going to a good home, to a man who will keep and treasure her as I did. That helps!"

I listened while he was talking furrowing his brows. His brown eyes became soft and he looked at me for some time.

"What do you see in this colt?" he asked me suddenly. He is handsome to be sure and he has auspicious markings, yet he is nothing special."

I shrugged. "I can't really explain it, it is more his character than his looks," I said. "He became my companion and friend and when I ride him, I am happy, it is as simple as that!'

"Then you should keep him," Anand told me gently. "Take him with you to Udaipur. He has little meaning for me and I doubt that I will find a buyer for him here, next year perhaps when he has grown a bit stronger and more muscled. And you will go back to Germany anyhow, right? So, tell Viru to send him back to me then."

"But you don't want any money from me?" I asked, incredulously.

"I am a horse lover, not a horse trader!" he said with humor twinkling in his eyes. "Besides, if you keep training him, he will only increase in value."

I was mum with shock and disbelief, but Anand had spoken in earnest.

I went to Suraj and told him in his ear, that he was mine now and that I would take him back to Udaipur with me. Suraj was quite unfazed by the news and continued munching his Luzern grass which had just been distributed to all the horses. I stayed with him for some time watching as he carefully picked up each strand of grass with his lips and chewed and swallowed it with apparent pleasure before attacking the next one. Slowly the big responsibility of owning and caring for a horse dawned on me and I grew quite solemn. Still, my heart was also filled with pride and happiness and I felt like bursting with joy.

Jay returned a little while later and asked me about my day. When he heard that Anand had given Suraj to me, he shook his head and asked me, "So how are you planning to take the horse first to Udaipur and then to Germany with you?"

He was a little annoyed yet strangely good-humored. He did not even listen to my answer but told me, "Well, I better go and arrange a truck for tomorrow and you go and buy whatever horse stuff you still need for your new horse. You know very well that there is nothing available in Udaipur!"

I did as he told me and bought a new halter, some brushes, and a leather bridle for my horse and then spent the rest of the day at the camp enjoying the new feeling of being a horse owner, knowing that tomorrow we all would go back to Udaipur, my new home.

We returned to Udaipur the following day but I never returned to Germany after my year in India was over. Jay and I became close and developed plans for our own farm and safari business. Ten months later we got married and bought a piece of land to build our dream on.

Suraj was the first horse to move there.

Joining the Equestrian Adventuresses Club

BY ELIZABETH WICKER

"That was not a circle," there was no denying it, but I couldn't speak. "That was around the edge of the arena." Again, irrefutable. The voice turns exasperated. "Liz, you need to canter a CIRCLE."

Trying not to cry, I tried a second time. I nudged Bracken into a trot, picked up the canter in the far corner, reached the next corner, came off the track, and then I lurched forward in terror and pulled her up into an unbalanced trot, gripping the front of the saddle tightly. The riding instructor's sigh was audible, but she didn't ask me to try again.

Nine years of sporadic riding lessons, and I just couldn't do it.

"Of course, you're riding with me," Lyra's expression was best described as perplexed. "Why wouldn't you?"

There were a variety of answers to that question, all along the same theme: I'm not a good enough rider, I'll slow her down and ruin her ride, I'm not confident enough to go haring off along Icelandic riverbeds.

I shrugged helplessly and looked vaguely anxious.

"You'll be fine."

I was a pony obsessed child. I had pony models, I rewrote the horse and pony adverts in the local village paper, I went to a local heavy horse center every year for my birthday, but my parents had three kids and couldn't afford horse-riding lessons. I rode my bike a lot and practiced standing up, no hands, ramps, and more, convinced that one day it would help my balance as a rider. Every time we went to zoos/farms and I could have a pony ride I did until I was queuing with my younger sister one day and realized with horror the girls leading the ponies around were my age. I put horses to the back of my mind (although I still had a poster of the black stallion on my wall and read every horse story) for the next few years.

At University, I signed up to loads of clubs and societies, including the equestrian society where I joined a few awkward socials—everyone else was an experienced rider, and there was me, a "pre-rider." I had a few riding lessons which I loved, there was a wonderful horse at the riding school called William, a tall, black ex-hunter that I did my first (completely terrifying) few strides of canter. I thought about riding constantly. I distinctly remember thinking about the rhythm of rising trot in a seminar when my tutor interrupted my daydream to ask me a question! But the riding school was a £10 taxi ride away and I just couldn't afford them for very long.

As riding lessons and equestrian society faded away and other things took their place, I was persuaded to go out with a flat mate for St. Paddy's day. At some point that night (my memory is hazy!) a short, fierce Irish girl I knew by sight bounded up to me and drizzled my face in green Celtic war paint. This girl turned out to be Lyra, my best friend, and initiator of many of my horse riding adventures, cheerleader, co-conspirator, and breeder of my pride and joy, my welsh cob mare, Nia.

Lyra lived near me in Wales with a cluster of dogs and horses, lovely welsh cobs, which I was chided most strongly for calling nice Irish ponies! Lyra encouraged me to start riding again, and when I did eventually, she was always on the other end of the phone. I rode sporadically for years, having lessons for a few months, then having to stop due to time/money shortfalls. I moved around the country a lot in my twenties, finding new riding schools whenever I moved.

And although I was riding a bit more often, I wasn't seeming to be improving, I don't think I improved any from those first riding lessons I had at 18 for the next 10 years. I could walk, trot and canter in a school, except never in a circle. I hated canter circles. I couldn't figure them out for the life of me, I always felt like I was going to be catapulted out the side door. Several times before lessons, I had a sick anxious feeling in my stomach and wondered why I was bothering.

I could pop a teeny cross pole if there was only one and it was built up from a trot pole! I'd been on the odd hack, walking and trotting were fine, but I hated cantering. I always felt completely out of control and a bit scared! I remember one time I was cantering at the back of a ride on this lovely little skewbald called Mel. She was about 15.2h and a gentle soul, and I was terrified of cantering her! My left leg started to go back. And go back...and go back until it was stretched out behind me and I looked like some weird Cossack. I was gripping on for dear life, luckily the ride leader saw I was doing my own stunts and called a halt.

In retrospect, despite the experiences that have shaped me since, I am disappointed I didn't enjoy riding more back then. This was when I was living in Wales, and the riding school had access to a local park full of sandy trails, perfect for cantering, within a coniferous forest and no roads for miles. The hacking where I live in England now just isn't the same!

I could have continued like that, loving horses, wanting desperately to be a "rider," feeling that I'd missed the boat and I should have started younger and why was I bothering when it scared me so much and I wasn't very good at it...until I went on a trip to Iceland (with Lyra and her husband) and met a cracking little horse called Valla. This was the trip that changed everything, or I should say it was the start of everything!

Iceland is singly the most beautiful country I have ever seen. As we drove away from the airport in the Dormobile—a 4WD that converted into a camper—I think we just stared and drank in the scenery. Hummocks of grass as far as the eye could see and hills and mountains in the distance. We stopped by a thundering waterfall to grab a bite to eat and we were surprised there was no one else there, amazing scenery is par for the course in Iceland!

Our first night we stayed at a small campsite five miles down a dirt track called an "F" road. In Iceland, they have "F" roads which are only suitable for four-wheel drives. Pak Gil, (pronounced "Thakgil") the campsite, is situated in a tiny bowl of a lush valley, surrounded on three sides by a large stream, with caves situated in the valley sides. These caves, which you cross a small wooden bridge to get to, are lined with candles and have long wooden tables and BBQs for you to cook and eat at. Our first proper meal in Iceland was hotpot Icelandic lamb and potatoes, seasoned with the arctic thyme that grows like a carpet underfoot. Lyra and I have been on a few camping trips together, and we like to eat well while roughing it! Up a small track from the campsite there is a small, deep pool fed by a glacial stream, we watched a pair of diving ducks reach the bottom of the pool to graze there; I don't think I've ever seen such clear, pure water before or since.

Pak Gil isn't far from the black sands of Vik which are eerily beautiful… just a flat expanse of black sands out to sea, overlooked by cliffs teeming with seagulls, including adorable portly puffins poking their stripy beaks out of their burrows and fulmars screaming on the wind.

If Iceland isn't thought of as a culinary destination, it should be. A few days into our trip we reached Höfn, a small town in the South East that is pronounced like a hiccough (HUP, en!). We pitched our camper and walked into the small town and found a restaurant not 10 meters from the fishing boat that supplied it. Here we ordered langoustines drizzled in rich garlicky butter, the biggest, tastiest, juiciest, and meatiest langoustines I have ever had in my life. Compared to our delicious UK ones that I've sampled in Loch Fyne, these were on another level! We also sampled the local beer, I forget the name, but it had arctic herbs in it and we all had very strong headaches after a tiny amount, it must have been stronger than we were used to (although it tasted delicious!).

In our culinary adventure, we managed one more local delicacy. We had concluded that we couldn't bring ourselves to try whale, we've both raised our own animals for meat and the most important thing to us is that our animals have happy lives and a quick, clean death. This is not something that is guaranteed with whale meat! We didn't have an opportunity to try Greenland shark, although Lyra's sister, who had traveled around Iceland the week before us described it as "it smells of cat pee and is kind of chewy." It is something that I may have to try on my return visit…

Our final delicacy was taken in Husavik, after we had spent the day on an old sailing ship watching humpback and minke whales feed in the runoff from waterfalls, before being treated to the spectacular sight of a pair of white-sided dolphins escorting the ship back to the harbor. We ate in a dark gloomy restaurant, and our starter was smoked puffin breast. All I can say is puffins are adorable on the outside and very, very tasty on the inside!

Obviously, we couldn't visit Iceland without meeting the Icelandic ponies! I had been given a book about them as a child, along with a book on Friesians and Andalusians, and it had been a secret wish of mine that I would get a chance to ride each of these breeds.

I expected to be riding with Lyra's husband, who I think has sat on a horse twice in his entire life, and leave Lyra to go on a speedy hack by herself. After all, I hated cantering on trails, hadn't been on a hack in over a year and I didn't want to ruin Lyra's ride. I still couldn't canter in a wretched circle! Lyra however was horrified by this. "Liz, you can ride! I don't know what you're worried about!" I was worried about everything.

But the day came around and we arrived at a small stable in the middle of an open plain. I was duly introduced to a sturdy grey mare, about 13h, called Valla. The three of us left, accompanied by two guides, and set off at a gentle walk. I was fine with this, I had enough faith to think I could trot, and maybe try this tölt I'd heard about as a kid and wanted to try (after all, it wasn't supposed to be much faster than a trot…?) but I wasn't keen on this whole cantering idea. There is a picture of me on Valla, a fixed grin in place, definitely one of those "I'm supposed to be enjoying this so I will pretend to!" moments.

We got to a point where the ride stopped, and Lyra's husband and his guide peeled off. This was the point of no return. Our guide grinned, "Shall we try a tölt?"

Her little piebald however balked at the idea of being the lead horse and Lyra switched to being in front. We stepped up into a trot. Lyra tried to find the tölt but ended going up a gear into a canter, and I (the guide) halted as she galloped off into the distance.

"I think she's gone."

The guide grinned and shrugged, "She looks like she can handle it! Shall we have another try?"

On the tiny crisscrossing sandy trails of the dried-up riverbed, the guide showed me how to position my seat and support their head and Valla switched into this incredible gliding pace, so smooth and comfortable I could have held a mug of tea and not spilled it.

Eventually, we caught up with Lyra who had wheeled around and rejoined us, and I was starting to enjoy myself. The views were incredible, we were in a huge riverbed/flood plain with mountains in the distance with the sun on our backs.

"Shall we canter?"

I winced but didn't disagree. And the strangest thing happened.

I was behind the guide, and my Valla was much faster than the little piebald, so much so her amazing extended trot was keeping pace with the piebald's canter and I had to continually ask Valla to maintain the distance. And I felt… disappointed. I hadn't even gone into a canter at that point, hated cantering on hacks, and here I was feeling a bit hard done by! The guide waved me past, shouting to stand up as I did. I jumped into a 2-point position and little Valla took off and I was hot on Lyra's heels. I can still remember the grin she gave me as she realized I was behind her. The "See, I knew you could do it" grin.

This wasn't gentle sedate cantering, this was a rag it canter, with tight turns and flat stretches where we could step up the pace! At one point we reached a fork in the trail and I followed Lyra left, only to hear the guide hollering, "Stop! There's a waterfall!" And indeed, there was. We slid to a stop, did a quick about-turn, and cantered a bit more gently back to the guide.

She was grinning at us, "You enjoyed that I think!" She laughed. "See, Mama Liz, your first experience of Irish hooligan riding! We should do this for a full holiday next time!"

The next trip was a year later, in Spain riding lovely flowy Andalusians (and another breed ticked off my wish list!). My horse was Muxu, a beautiful bay Andalusian with a lovely soft nose. "Muxu" means "kisses" in Basque and he certainly had a few of these! This was a farm-based stay where we rode out on different trails for the week, and I was sick to my stomach before the first ride out. This wasn't helped within the first five minutes, Muxu decided he'd had enough of my anxious riding and decided to whizz around and try and head back to the farm! So, then I was anxious and mortified! However, after the first canter—his smooth, rolling canter that was a dream to sit to—I started to get a bit more confident.

Muxu showed me two things: the difference between a collected canter and a faster gallop, and he showed how I could switch between the two by changing my seat position slightly. The second thing was that as we were charging at a fast canter downhill, I had to sit up and take some control of the pace! This trip gave me an amazing confidence boost.

The food was very delicious too. One night we were treated to a mammoth bowl of squid ink pasta, a salty, rich dish with a faint after-taste of iodine. It was just the thing to fill us up after a full day of riding!

Two years later, we were on the last day of our trail ride in Croatia, a whizzy trail with loads of long canters on a lovely little mare called Olympia. Our guide wanted some film footage of us, the last guests of the season. He parked his horse in the center of a large grassy space and gestured us to ride around him in a large circle.

"You canter, yes? I film."

I had to laugh. "You want me to canter in a circle? No problem."

Croatia was another place where the food was memorable. Every dinner we had, we were served a bowl each of fresh cabbage or lettuce. The first night, it wasn't touched, but by the end of the week, after days of long rides, they were being demolished! I haven't looked that forward to a starter since. The local red wines were also very addictive, cheap, cheerful, and very easy to drink!

After these trips, especially the fast trail ride in Croatia, if it sounds like I had turned overnight into this confident, self-assured rider, this is misleading. The confidence ebbed and flowed depending on the time of day! It still does to this day, although today I am much better at snapping out of any negative spirals.

A big boost to my confidence came from what was supposed to be a short afternoon ride. My partner and I were on holiday in Dalyan, a small town on a river in Turkey, not far from Dalaman airport. The town is on the south side of the river, opposite a cliff with tombs carved into it. The way to the beach is a slow trip on a riverboat through the reeds where the African Queen was allegedly filmed. The beach is sandy, busy, and windy in the afternoons making big waves. Every time we went, we saw loggerhead turtles.

The town itself is lovely, with lots of shops and restaurants, some of which are on the river itself, and if you're sat there at dusk you can watch the bats streaming overhead and feeding on the bugs that fly over the river. There are lots of companies offering excursions, some I'd already done like Saklikent gorge. One place offered horse rides and over the week I went from not being interested, "Who wants to sit in a group with non-riders and plod..." (Because now, I was a RIDER, maybe not a very good rider, but a rider nonetheless!) to, "might be nice riding a horse in another country" to "shall I just book it?"

And so, I booked a two, hour plod, starting at 4 pm (because I thought it would be cooler by then). I had no hat, body protector, jodhpurs, or boots. Since it was going to be a gentle walk, I figured loose cotton harem pants, a white kaftan and plimsolls would be ok (luckily, I had a sports bra handy!). My other half doesn't ride so I was going solo.

Mark and I were waiting on the hotel steps where a Renault that was older than me pulled up outside. The hotel barman was watching. "You ride with Kudret? He's my neighbor, a very good man!"

Thus reassured, and not for the last time, I let a strange man drive me into the middle of nowhere to go riding. We drove to a pomegranate orchard, parked in the middle of it, and set off to meet the horses. They were separated and ground tied, some hard to see because of the height of the grass. After I helped Kudret separate a colt and a mare tangled up together, he stopped, looked me up and down, and asked, "You ride?"

"Yes."

"You ride good? Gallop?"

"Well yes, but…"

"You ride a white horse, he very fast."

So I was given a 15h-ish grey gelding called Yildiz. We led him to the village, (I being the only guest) Kudret tacked up the horses and set off. One of my concerns was my feet slipping through the stirrups, but they were caged stirrups, so it wasn't an issue. I tried not to think about my unprotected head.

We set off at a clip through the village where I found that Turkish Rahvan horses don't trot, they pace, which I couldn't rise or sit to. Kudret also told me a little bit more about Yildiz, some not exactly reassuring. As a stallion he had been a nutcase, so they had him castrated and now he was a lot more—not exactly relaxed or calm, although he spooked at nothing—just "not crazy" as he was quite happy to have me on his back. He just liked to go fast and faster yet responded to my seat quickly. The only issue we had at the start was I was holding my reins "properly." Kudret showed me the one-handed grip, a bit like how you hold the reins in polo and after that, we got on brilliantly. The only time he told me to watch out was when we were going over a ditch and he warned Yildiz might jump, trouble was he told me as I was mid-air, so now I can add jumping without a hat to the list of things I shouldn't have done!

After hammering down some roads and tracks, Kudret pulled up and gestured at a pipe with water pouring out. He explained it was spring water, used to irrigate the poly-tunnels in the adjacent field. He gave me his horse's reins, lay down on the ground, and put his face in the water flow. Then he asked me if I was thirsty. As I was gasping at that point, I said yes, jumped off Yildiz, and did the same. As I got up, he was wearing a perplexed expression holding a water bottle out for me. I laughed and asked if he saw many English girls do that, he replied, "No, today you are crazy Turkish horse girl."

We cantered down more tracks alongside fields and through orchards, he paused to scrimp some limes. As we passed a house, a woman and her two daughters waved, we pulled up and gave the girls horse rides, me encouraging the horses from behind as they followed Kudret, then went back to the house for a delicious Turkish coffee while Kudret caught up with his friends. I was passed the baby as soon as I brought the girls back and had some lovely photos with the family, none of whom could speak English but we smiled a lot while Kudret and the Grandfather talked!

As we left, Kudret said he couldn't do that with most tourists. It was a nice window into real Turkey.

Then we galloped up to the rocky outcrop overlooking the lake, arriving 5 seconds after the sun slid behind the mountain. We stopped for fresh melon and water, letting the horses loose to graze. People were swimming off a boat on the lake below, we could hear the music, and ducks settling in for the night. As we'd already been two hours and I was supposed to be at the hotel, I gave Mark a ring to let him know I was ok.

By the time we got back, including a "no-hands" canter race, a mad pace on the roads in the pitch black, and a final canter through a pomegranate orchard where I couldn't see Kudret's horse in front! (I may have said a prayer at that point), we arrived back at Kudret's village. Leaving the horses with nose bags, Kudret drove me at a breakneck pace in his ancient banger. When I protested, or he saw me turn green, he explained he didn't want to get me into trouble with Mark, which was sweet (Mark is well used to me disappearing for hours with horses!). Mark was there to greet us, and I was somewhat surprised when he gave Kudret a tip (in addition to the one I'd already given).

We waved him off and Mark said, "From the way you sounded on the phone, you either had the best ride of your life or the best ride of your life, either way, he probably deserved a tip!"

So, after a wonderful trip to Turkey, I decided it was time to put my brave pants on. Lyra couldn't make a holiday that year, so I was riding solo. I had decided to go to Morocco, it seemed good value for money, it was an opportunity to ride a stallion, and while I'm not fussed about riding destination as long as it's somewhere new and the horses were special, I knew Lyra would never pick Morocco as her first choice.

So, after a lot of agonizing, emailing the holiday agent if she was sure I thought I would cope, I found myself heading away from Essaouria airport with a French-speaking taxi man on my own. The next day would see me picked up and driven to the stables, paired up with a stallion and heading inland, camping every night until the circuit brought us back to Essaouria. To say my heart was in my mouth was an understatement.

After a somewhat sleepless night in the riad, we headed to the stables. I'd met one guest on the ride the night before, and I was introduced to the rest on the ride over.

Our hosts were French Marie and her Moroccan partner, and my nerves were not put at rest when Marie went through the safety briefing, remember they're stallions, keep your distance because they will kick, don't give them treats because they won't respect you, keep the rein contact always….I was probably green by this point. What on Earth had I signed up to?!

Then Marie asked if there were any nervous riders, I told her I was nervous until I got on, and then I was usually fine. She relayed this to her partner in French who duly pointed out Salim, a grey stallion about 15.3 hands. He had an amazingly quiet, dignified presence.

I mounted and sat getting used to the feel of the saddle, acclimatizing to the fact I was sitting on a stallion! As we started riding off, I was towards the back as Salim didn't like horses behind him and I could see one guest having a bad time of it, her horse was plunging and leaping all over the place, trying to take off with her.

This did not make me feel any better, especially when one of the guides mounted the horse and the guest was driven in the jeep to the first lunch point.

More warnings followed, be careful going down sand dunes as the horses like to roll…

Salim didn't even try to roll. I was still nervous but felt myself loosening up as we walked. I had a few small trots where I could get used to the feel of him (he was a very comfortable horse) and then when the guide and I stopped to take pictures, I had a little canter to catch up with the others. He was so responsive, I'd like to think I relaxed then, but it came and went throughout the holiday.

There was a lovely moment when the group was making its way down a slope to go up the other side. A gap had appeared, and as I was on the flat and the uphill track looked wide and smooth, I had a little canter up it. Salim stretched his legs out to take off but with a small adjustment in the saddle (it was literally nothing, I just sat up a little) he collected himself beautifully and I had the nicest canter and he stopped on a dime when asked. One guest following me said, "That looked beautiful, you were so in tune!" It remains one of the nicest things I've ever had anyone say about my riding!

This trip also gave me my favorite post-riding snack of all time: dark chocolate, dried fruits (figs and dates and apricots), and nuts. I always have a mix of stashed in my cupboard now. We always had a platter to share after a day's ride, to tide us over until dinner time, served with a refreshing cup of hot mint tea.

Another special moment with Salim was when we were galloping on the beach, we already had two long gallops by then and I was knackered. So, I asked Salim to pull back to a canter while the other horses went on ahead. We had a lovely calm canter through the waves, the others were specs in the distance! When we caught up to the others, one of the guides pointed out that his dog had been faster than us. I laughed; Salim was fantastic. The gallops themselves were breathless, I have never been on a horse as fast before or since! Finally, I felt like I'd joined this "riders club" that had eluded me since I was a kid.

My latest adventure is owning a welsh cob (part welsh dragon obviously) who I am re-starting myself. I don't think I've done too badly for a girl who was afraid of cantering in a circle...

As for mine and Lyra's next trip, we've already planned it. We're off to Kyrgyzstan on another riding adventure!

Show Jumping in Italy

BY ASHLEY BEALL

In August of 2016, my family and I moved from Loveland, Colorado in the United States to Rome, Italy. Although throughout my life I had loved to travel and had the fondest memories of Italy, the idea of living in a foreign country overwhelmed me. But what overwhelmed me most was probably not what one might expect. My biggest fear was that I would spend the three years that we were scheduled to be in Rome living strictly as a tourist. I wanted to learn about and experience Italy from Italians as a local.

I was anxious and concerned that because I am an extroverted introvert, and most importantly did not speak Italian, I would allow myself to spend my days with fellow Americans sheltered from the genuine Italian lifestyle. Or worse, that I would be intimidated and pause my life completely. Therefore, as an avid equestrian who was found in the irons daily, I decided before the move to challenge myself to continue to ride, to set once-in-a-lifetime goals, and pursue my passion in Italy.

Our housing had been assigned a few weeks before our arrival. Knowing that traffic was an issue in Rome and not wanting to spend hours in my car, I researched show jumping training stables located near the apartment building where my family would be living. I found what appeared to be a few great stables. A few days after my plane landed at the Rome- Fiumicino International Airport, and after meeting my children's teachers on the first day of school, I headed directly to Circolo Ippico Vigna Clara. (For those performing the same research, it wasn't called Circolo Ippico Vigna Clara. I've changed the names to protect the innocent!)

I was too excited to wait another day. As I entered the gates of the stable, I considered maybe I should have called to make an appointment. But I was already there. I walked through the gate separating the parking lot from the stable, my heart racing. I attempted to introduce myself to the first person who crossed my path. She quickly redirected me to a man named Stefano. Stefano's English was almost perfect. A feeling of relief swept over me. I later learned that his mother was British and his father was Italian.

I detailed my riding history and future goals to him. He provided me with an overview of the stable, then introduced me to Fulvio. Fulvio was the owner and head trainer/instructor at Vigna Clara and did not speak English.

Stefano translated our introduction. Fulvio nodded throughout, then walked away.

Feeling awkward and confused, I requested a lesson with Stefano. He then informed me that he was the intermediate instructor. Based upon my level of riding, Stefano explained that all of my lessons would be with Fulvio. He further explained that the stable did not have adequate lesson horses available for advanced riders. All advanced riders must own their horse.

This made perfect sense to me, however, I considered my scenario unique. I had no plans to ship my horse to Europe. I had decided months before to board my horse at my friend's stable in Colorado for the three years that I would be living in Rome. I planned to first establish a relationship with a trainer/instructor and then, after settling in our new digs, to purchase a horse. But as Stefano explained it, I must have a horse to be accepted into the training program. More confused than ever, I stood there in silence staring blankly at the riders schooling in the ring. I wondered if I should thank Stefano and make a swift exit.

The next stable on my list was only a few miles to the east. Eventually, Stefano broke the silence. He suggested that I book a "prova" or test with Fulvio to showcase my riding abilities. If I impressed, he expounded, Fulvio might be willing to make an exception. So English or not, I did just that.

Three days later I returned for my prova and was greeted with less than enthusiasm. Fulvio said, "Ciao" and pointed at a horse. I searched awkwardly for Stefano until I noticed a groom rushing to prepare the horse. As he did so I tied my hair back and tucked it neatly inside my helmet. The groom walked the horse to the mounting block and held the reins as I mounted.

I quietly said, "grazie," and entered the ring. As I nervously walked along the rail, I noticed Fulvio motioning to me. He checked the tightness of my girth and instructed me to demonstrate my abilities, at least that's what I thought he said in Italian. That was it. My mind raced. I slowly started to trot, then began more forward movement and encouragement of a frame.

After 30 or so minutes, Fulvio motioned again for me. He complimented the softness of my hands and pointed at a vertical jump that measured no more than a meter. I jumped it from both directions. That was it. Then I waited and waited. After a few days, I contacted Stefano, curious about the next step. Fulvio had not decided. I returned twice. Each time Fulvio was slightly friendlier and snuck in an additional English word or two. Finally, he had decided. I must purchase a horse. A horse named Arita. His horse. And I had to commit to riding every day.

I spent the next few weeks riding Arita trying to determine if this was the horse for me. As I had only lived in Rome a few weeks, the thought of purchasing a horse made me anxious. My household items, my bed, our pots and pans, the majority of our clothes, had yet to arrive from the US. I had just a few priorities before purchasing a horse. After all, I had to continue to schedule my lessons with Fulvio through WhatsApp with Stefano even though it was becoming more evident that Fulvio DID speak English. Most days I felt as though I was a mere inconvenience for Fulvio, but it was also starting to feel like I was his payday. Arita was not an easy horse. But, my desperation to ride dominated my thoughts. I purchased Arita.

For the next two months, I spent almost every day with Fulvio. He taught six days a week and was extremely involved in my horse's daily training and care. He was excited for Arita and I to compete. He offered to contact the Italian Federation of Equestrian Sports (FISE) on my behalf to coordinate the purchase of my license. A license? I was extremely confused. I considered that Fulvio's explanation of the license was lost in translation. I had completed the necessary US Equestrian application forms to renew my USEF and USHJA memberships. I assumed that a guest license was similar in that it was a fee-based membership.

But I was wrong. I soon learned that in Italy, as is the case in many European countries, you must be issued a level-based license to compete. I learned that I must complete and submit to the United States Equestrian Federation (USEF) a National Permission Questionnaire.

Within two days I received an e-mail notification from the USEF and a copy of the letter sent to FISE. The letter confirmed that I had competed up to 1.20 meters.

A few days later, Fulvio informed me that I was granted a "Brevetto" license. A Brevetto license allowed me to compete in classes 1.0 – 1.15 meters in height. As I had previously competed up to 1.20 meters, I was confused. I had expected to be granted a Primo Grado license which would allow me to compete in classes 1.15 - 1.35 meters in height. Fulvio explained that because I had not competed at 1.35 meters, FISE could not grant me a Primo Grado.

I struggled with this concept and was extremely frustrated. To be granted the next grade of a license, a rider must accrue a number of points and pass horsemanship examinations in Italy, in Italian. But basically, a rider must have proven results at the heights. I had proven results up to 1.20 meters.

I would have argued that one would have had competed at 1.15 and 1.10 successfully before competing at 1.20 meters. Fulvio assured me that he did everything he could and that I should not be deterred. He was confident I would quickly earn enough points to be granted a Primo Grado license. He did not share my apprehension that I would languish at these low heights and never be able to compete at the heights I wanted to before my three years were up.

I did my best to stay focused. I continued to train daily with Fulvio and in early February, at my first competition with Arita, I was extremely excited. I was there to win. My husband had invited a few of our American neighbors. We competed in the 1.10 class. I precisely walked the most efficient pathway along the course. I was feeling confident. But when I mounted Arita I could feel her nervous energy. I struggled to control her as she raced to each jump in the warm-up. The day did not go as planned. We ended with 15 faults.

Arita and I continued to compete together for the next three months with varying results. It got worse before better. Just when I felt Arita and I had begun meshing, I decided to invite some new Italian friends we had recently met to a competition. At each of the first three jumps of the course, I could hear cheers from my very vocal Italian friend, sometimes in English and sometimes a stout "Brava!" or "Grande!" That was until Arita and I had a disagreement at a jump where I said go and she said NO! I landed square on my back in the middle of a jump, Arita looking down at me with this quizzical expression of why I was in the dirt looking up at her.

Needing to gain a little confidence, I decided to attend a three-day competition in Narni. After a challenging first day attempting to wrangle Arita's wild spirit, she stepped out of her stall calm on day two. The clouds parted, and she won with ease against tough competition. On day three, she placed third. Finally, we were a cohesive team. I was optimistic and confident about our future together.

Horses have a way of keeping us humble, and unfortunately a week after returning to Rome, Arita appeared to be lame. Following the veterinarian's examination of her, my heart broke. She had a deep digital flexor tendon injury. The vet had seen only three cases previously in his career. Her prognosis was not great, and although it was unlikely that she would return to competition, I held tight to the slight chance she could be rehabilitated.

I spent eight months painstakingly nursing Arita back to health. I spent months walking by her side, and then I returned to the saddle and slowly increased the work. Eventually, I concluded that although I had developed an unbreakable bond with Arita, and desperately wanted her to be with me to achieve my goals, it was unrealistic. Arita's health was more important. I talked with Fulvio and he agreed. Therefore, Fulvio and I began searching for my next partner and a home for Arita as a broodmare.

I did not have to try many horses until Fulvio had found his dream horse. I was not convinced. Well, I was not convinced that this was the horse of my dreams. But, as our relationship had strengthened, I chose to trust Fulvio.

Funny though, as we were negotiating the price of the new horse, I learned that I never officially owned Arita. Fulvio had retained ownership. He had deemed it too difficult to change ownership over to me. Was it too difficult? Was he just being lazy? Was he trying to pull one over on the American who didn't know how to navigate purchasing a horse in Italy? If I hadn't seen documents showing Arita was still his, would he have ever told me? If I wanted to take Arita back to the US, would it have even been possible? Could I trust this man that either saw enough talent or dollar signs to miraculously learn English in a matter of weeks as I became a regular fixture at his barn? Was this a man I could trust with the next investment of my heart and checkbook?

I already had the feeling he was pushing me to compete to bring prestige to his barn and his name; the Italian who could make an American win in Italy. The Italians have this neat little word that doesn't have an exact translation or at least a short one suggested by such a short word: "furbo." Furbo means sneaky, willing to go to great lengths to get what one wants even if those lengths are questionable, legally, and/or morally. Fulvio was Furbo.

I purchased Quiralido in November. And this time I was sure of it, invoice, passport, the whole nine yards to prove I actually had ownership. Fulvio was hopeful we would be show ready in two weeks. Two weeks! He was anxious for me to again accrue points towards my license. But Quiralido, "Q," was a very different horse than Arita. Arita was complicated. She charged the jumps. Q is a more straight-forward, consistent horse. I should have welcomed his efforts, but I continually anticipated Arita's energy burst three strides before the fence. I struggled to adjust to him. I hesitated to create pace. I developed a terrible habit of circling when I did not see a distance to the fence. I was, for the first time, fearful. I was fearful I would be less than perfect and that I would disappoint Fulvio. Fulvio had such high expectations of Q and most days I questioned if I was fit to showcase his abilities. I was always reminiscing to Fulvio about Arita, trying to sell the idea I would amaze if partnered with her.

The truth though, was that Arita was difficult to ride. Mistakes happened. We had inconsistent results in competitions. She was one of the most fun horses to ride. We developed an unbreakable bond. However, she had more often than not, a certain dragon-like quality. I was living in an imaginary past and was holding myself back from success.

Accepting the mental aspect of this sport and my struggle to live up to expectations, I forced myself to acknowledge the talents of Q. Time continued to pass as I fought with myself to learn and grow from my mistakes. I had not yet registered Q and with only one show to end the year, it was wasteful to pay an annual registration fee. I set my sights on January. The first week of the new year, I again completed and submitted to USEF a National Permission Questionnaire. As expected, I was granted an international guest Brevetto license.

Fulvio planned an intense winter schedule. Q and I continued to struggle. Fulvio would constantly say, "This horse will amaze." We worked together with Q six days a week through January. Riders would comment almost daily on how impressed they were. But, I had yet to develop a bond with Q, and to add complication, I wanted to be perfect. The pressure was mounting.

Then, in February, my father unexpectedly passed away. I withdrew from the stable completely. I traveled to the United States twice in the following three months. But I spent most days with my American friends or in my apartment binge-watching TV. Eventually, after four or five weeks, I returned to the stable. It felt like a chore. I felt like an outsider. I had no interest in competing. I attempted to explain how I was feeling to Fulvio. He thought I was scared of the horse. Maybe I was. I was definitely scared of failing, of spending every day surrounded by strangers and achieving nothing in three years.

I wasn't having fun. That should have been the point of all of this, shouldn't it? Disengaged from everyone, I walked along the rail one day after a lesson. A girl returning to a walk from a canter came alongside me. Half-laughing, she questioned if I would ever compete with my horse. She went further to suggest that she ride him. I was insulted. My father had passed away only months earlier. My family and I were living in a country far from everyone important to us. It was none of her business. But, it proved to be a challenge I was desperate to accept. Later that day I messaged Fulvio. I was ready to return to the show ring right then and there.

Almost eight months after purchasing Q, we competed in our first competition. We competed over three days and he was absolutely perfect. I returned home with ribbons and a renewed excitement. I was confident that a year was time enough to accomplish my goals and I could not wait until our next competition.

With an amazing first show and little time to waste, I was thinking big. I wanted to compete internationally. Not only was this a pre-set goal of mine, but in an international competition, I did not have the license constraints. Fulvio began planning and scheming. I decide to vacation with my family and friends early that summer so I would have ample time to travel around Europe competing with Q. On our last day of vacation, Fulvio, in anticipation of my return, called to discuss the schedule with me. He had grand plans. He wanted to focus on competitions in Spain and France. I said, "Yes!" to all of it. I could hardly wait to return to Rome. That night I enjoyed a magnificent dinner with friends. I was happy. I remember thinking that it couldn't be a more perfect evening. Everything was as I had wanted it. As I had dreamt it!

Exhausted from what had been a perfect day, I returned to the hotel after dinner. It was late at night and my youngest son had fallen asleep. He was way past the age of carrying, and I was wearing heels, but I figured I'd do him the favor because of the long fun-filled day we had. Lost in thought as I walked from my car to the entrance of the hotel, I was startled. I heard screaming. Then, laughter. Flashlights were slashing across the night sky like mini searchlights. I focused forward to see three men chasing a big black shadow in my direction. As it got closer and bigger, there was just enough light I could recognize the silhouette of a huge wild boar barreling toward me.

Jumping out of the beast's path I hit a hole and fell. As I landed, I heard a pop. The hotel employees who were chasing the boar stopped as they came upon me, on the ground with a crying seven-year-old on top of me. They did the best they could to help me back to my room. The hotel manager even came in with a meager offering in a plastic bag. "We have ice," was about the extent of his English.

As scheduled the next day, I returned to Rome. As I could not bear weight, I went to the hospital to have my ankle x-rayed. The news was not good. I had a spiral fracture to my fibula. I was scheduled to have surgery the next day. My friends joked that my post-surgery x-ray looked like "Frankenfoot". I think Fulvio was more devastated than I was.

I spent two months out of the saddle. The first week of September, when Q returned to Rome from vacationing in Calabria, I started riding. Yes, even the horses have a vacation in August like every good Italian!

The first few days, Fulvio would first ride Q and I would walk the rail post-workout for 20 minutes. But, two years had already passed and I had goals, come hell or high water! So, I decided to ride. In just a few weeks, I was back in the show ring. But don't get me wrong, when I forced weight into my heel it was painful. More than once, I exited the arena in tears. It was decided by the orthopedic surgeon, myself, and Fulvio to remove the metal as quickly as possible. In December, five months after my first surgery, I had a second surgery to remove the metal.

In January, with only six months remaining in Rome, I renewed my USEF and USHJA memberships and completed the National Permission Questionnaire. The dates had changed but the letter was the same. It stated I had competed at a height up to 1.20 meters. As expected, I was granted a Brevetto license. Fulvio and I exchanged e-mails and had lengthy phone conversations with FISE. I was extremely frustrated. I felt hopeless.

I vented to one of the beginner instructors at Vigna Clara. She was dumbfounded. She had previously lived in Sweden where she competed up to 1.20 meters. When she moved to Italy, where her father and step-family lived, she was granted an Italian Primo Grado license to compete. I was shocked. I did not understand how this was possible. She simply went to the FISE Lazio office in Rome with her previous show records from Sweden, proving she had competed up to 1.20 meters, and was immediately granted the license. I went directly to Fulvio with this information. He, thinking that we had exhausted every avenue, thought I had misunderstood.

With only a few months remaining, I decide again to focus my attention on international competition. In international competition, I would ride under the rules and regulations of FEI and the USEF and therefore, could compete in classes with fence height exceeding 1.15 meters. The only problem, my horse did not have an international passport. The easiest and quickest way to upgrade his passport was through Italy. There were several necessary steps to achieve this. First, Fulvio and I gathered all documents showing I had ownership of Quiralido.

The next day we went to the FISE Lazio office located in Rome. I, to this day, do not understand the necessity of this additional step, but I am thankful that we did. While we were there to do whatever it was we were there to do, Fulvio casually questions what license I should be granted if I had competed at 1.20 meters previously in the United States.

The woman quickly without glancing in our direction responded with, "una patente Primo Grado."

Fulvio winked at me as he handed the woman my letter. He then offered me candy, I felt like a kid in a doctor's clinic and began chatting with everyone in the office. He was smiling and laughing. They were speaking quickly and I understood only parts of their conversations. I quickly distracted myself returning texts to avoid inclusion in the conversation. My Italian language skills were weak at best, and I was not looking to completely embarrass myself. From what I gathered they were discussing arena footing. They definitely were not discussing me. I continued to check the time, wondering why we were there.

Finally, Fulvio announced that we must go. The woman returned all of Q's documents and I rushed to join Fulvio as he exits. As soon as we are outside of the building and the door had shut behind us, Fulvio danced wildly with his entire body. I had never witnessed movement like this from him. I too was happy to be moving forward toward my goals, but Fulvio was elated.

I had not yet started my car when Fulvio called me. He was talking so rapidly, I could not understand him. I attempted to grasp at single words. Then, my husband texted. Fulvio had texted him. It was official, I had been granted a Primo Grado license. It was that easy. Two years had passed, two years! Maybe being furbo isn't so bad after all! The next day I, armed with my best Italian language skills, walked into the Olympic offices.

After an hour, and probably an embarrassing attempt to speak Italian, I had Quiralido's international passport. I think I was most proud of myself that I had braved this Italian experience completely solo. I had walked into the building filled with self-doubt but walked out with what I came for. Was I one step further from my fear of living strictly as a tourist?

Now with six months to go, I had no obstacles. This was it! I had completed all of the documents. I was armed with Q's international passport, a Primo Grado license that permitted me to compete in Italian competitions where international guests were not permitted and I was healthy and fit. I no longer felt like a stranger and many of the riders at Vigna Clara and I had developed genuine friendships. I was presented with a Vigna Clara club jacket and Q was outfitted with a fly bonnet, saddle pad, and a cooler for competition emblazoned with the barn logo. Was I officially a member of the team?!

Many of the people that rode at Vigna Clara had worked extremely hard to earn their licenses. A few of them, too, had struggled with setbacks. At our first show after being granted the Primo Grado license, I was extremely nervous. I was concerned about what everyone would think if I competed in the 1.20 with disastrous results. I did my best to push those thoughts aside. It was only 5 centimeters from 1.15 to 1.20. I could not allow myself to make a fuss. I did deserve this! I had the show records to prove my success at 1.15. I entered the ring, took a deep breath, and enjoyed the ride. Q was again perfect. He continued to impress throughout the weekend.

With only a few weeks remaining and now international experience, I set my sights on the Regional Horse Championship in Rome. It is a three-day competition where you are ranked on your cumulative score. I competed in the Primo Grado, 1.20. There were three of us representing Vigna Clara in the 1.20 class.

On the first day, Q jumped with zero faults. On the second day, Q rocked, jumping double clear. We entered the third day in 9th place out of an extremely competitive group of horse/rider combinations. Unfortunately for Fulvio and the stable, the two other riders representing Vigna Clara had accrued too many faults in the two previous days to be competitive. They continued on the third day but were without podium consideration.

As the order of go was in reverse order, Q and I were one of the last horse/rider combinations. I watched anxiously as 30 or so of my friends and fellow competitors navigated the course. Then, it was time to start preparing Q.

Once Q was warmed-up, we headed to the arena. I was discussing last-minute details with Fulvio when the rider on the course had an unfortunately abrupt dismount. She required ambulance assistance. We waited almost 30 minutes before I heard my name announced over the loudspeaker.

My heart raced. I was overwhelmed by my nerves. This would be my final competition in Italy. I was currently in 9th place. I had to quickly remind myself that this was not a challenge I was facing alone. I had Q. I had to learn to trust him, and that bond I was so desperate to build was stronger than I imagined it could be.

I entered the ring and took a deep breath as I heard the bell, then Fulvio yelling for me to "Come on." I galloped around the arena on my approach to the first fence, only to watch another competitor jump fence one. Completely frustrated, I continued to gallop while being mindful of the rider on course. As the rider galloped through the timers, I took another deep breath.

Finally, it was my time to ride. After a quick apology from the announcer, the bell. I galloped towards the first fence. There was complete silence as I swiftly navigated the course until Q hit a rail on fence 10B. I could hear the collective groans from the crowd echo with disappointment as I galloped toward fence 11, the final fence. Up, over, and through the timers. The crowd cheered loudly. The cheers were so loud that I glanced at 10B to confirm the pole had hit the dirt. I cantered around the arena toward the gate where Fulvio was standing. He smiled and playfully threw his hands in the air. As I exited the arena, he said, "Bad luck."

Overall, I finished the competition in 10th place. After the awards ceremony as I walked with my family to our car, one of my competitors congratulated me. She detailed her rounds in

English. I had known her for three years and had never heard her speak English. Had I finally earned everyone's respect? That night my friend sent me the video of my final round. Oddly enough, my favorite moment was when the crowd groans as the top rail rolls from the cups. It was as if everyone there was rooting for me. I realized then that I had not been alone on this journey. That I was no longer simply "The American," but was now considered a friend to many of my competitors.

The challenges were great and there were many days when I struggled to believe my goals were attainable. I often questioned my abilities. I questioned why I could not be happy enough binge-watching American television when my family and I weren't playing "tourist." But through it all, I ultimately prevailed. And I am so thankful that I did. It was truly one of the most challenging experiences, but the most irreplaceable journey of my life.

Riding with Toddlers: Trial & Error in Argentina

BY ANGELA MILLI

Spring was beginning at El Bolson, Argentina in October. It was wet, cold, and green around. Our 9-months-old daughter was making her first steps, while our 2-years-old son was carrying sticks for the fire. We just bought our third horse for the great trip we've been planning for a long time. As a family of four, we wanted to cross Latin America on horseback over the next ten years. It was an idea that seemed crazy to our friends and relatives considering the fact that we have two small children.

The beginning was very difficult and messy, we were getting to know the country and learning how much patience we need to do something here. When you come from a place as organized as Europe, it takes a while to understand that time in Argentina works differently and you just have to accept it. Being a foreigner with a basic knowledge of Spanish does not work in your favor either.

It felt like we'll never be able to leave as every day was bringing some small or big problems. Right at the beginning, our horse Malu got attacked by wild dogs and while trying to escape, he cut his chest deeply with a rope. A huge piece of skin was hanging out, 5 people had to hold Malu pinned down to the ground whilst our friend - a human doctor sewed his chest. He recovered fully, after two months you could barely see anything. At that time, it felt like it's the end of the journey which hasn't even started yet.

Then there's the story about how Malu became our packhorse. Malu was mistreated by one of the gauchos in the past, thus developed a fear of people and had trust issues. We hoped that with time and good care he'd be a great companion. He had a really good conformation of a sturdy, perfectly built Criollo. I only managed to ride him once, before we decided it's never going to happen again. And that was after my partner Mo, fell off his back and lost his memory for three days. Malu just went crazy when Mo was getting on him.

Mo wasn't even sitting in the saddle yet when Malu started running. Although he managed to hold on for quite a long time, eventually he fell and must have hit something hard. Next thing I know, he's in shock and keeps asking me questions and not remembering the answer after 30 seconds. He scared me a lot, imagine what I would do alone in Argentina with two children and three horses if he wouldn't recover.

I couldn't honestly picture it in my head, how the expedition will look like having two little kids. My partner seemed more confident and was reassuring me that he has everything worked out. We used to be crazy travelers before we had children, Mo stayed pretty much the same in his heart, but I've changed a lot. I wasn't willing to take any risks and all I cared about was the safety of our children. That's why the beginning was a huge adapting process, more for me than for my children Iyan & Ingis.

Kids have amazing adjusting capabilities and they're going to be happy anywhere, as long as they're fed, loved, and comfortable. They've been having fun right from the start, full of energy to explore new pieces of land, they would sit on the ground and dig holes or make drawings with a stick in the mud. I started to have a new understanding of the word "dirty." Whatever seemed dirty to me before, was now our normal state. There was no point in getting frustrated over the way their clothes looked like every day. I just had to accept it and move my usual standards of cleanliness.

We were finally ready to leave the campsite in El Bolson and start heading South with our two riding horses, a packhorse, and a motorbike with a trailer as support. The first day we'll always remember, as nothing went according to the plan. Whatever could go wrong, it went wrong.

It took us 4 hours to pack all our belongings in the morning and we had to abandon lots of things due to the lack of space. We only did 6 km walking with the horses, moving basically to the other side of El Bolson. Too tired to continue, we set up a camp and when everything was ready, a very unhappy neighbor called the police. We did ask other neighbors whether we can camp here and it was okay. This piece of land didn't belong to any of them… but the police asked us to move. Mo went on the motorbike to look for some other place and got bitten by a dog. He had to go to the hospital, while myself, the kids and horses, with the help of local people, went to an organized campsite.

So how did we do it with two little children? Iyan, our son would ride a horse for a while, with me or Mo next to him as a support, then he would go on a motorbike. Ingis, our daughter was too little to ride, although if I put her in the saddle just to take a picture, I won't be able to take her down. With her whole strength, she would hold on to the pommel and laugh. She is a true adventuress, not afraid of anything! She develops amazing relationships with animals and even though so little, she's much more easygoing than her older brother.

Ingis had a special baby carrier in which she was sitting, either while walking with horses or driving a motorbike. I and Mo would swap in riding horses and driving the bike.

We were also having volunteers to help us out with daily duties in exchange for horseback expedition experience. Since we had two riding horses, we could have one additional person traveling with us. So, most of the time, but not always, someone was joining our journey. They would help with setting up camp, looking after horses and in return got about 5 hours daily time spent in the saddle.

Driving a motorbike with children definitely wouldn't be acceptable in Europe and other more developed parts of the world, but it wasn't surprising here in Argentina. We've seen how a whole family can fit on a little scooter. I'm not sure whether it's legal or not, as police have seen us too many times with both children driving and didn't say a word about it, but in one village they wanted to give us a fine. But leaving all legalities behind, how did we ensure the safety of our children while driving? The trailer behind the motorbike was a modified bicycle trailer for children, which I brought with us from Europe. It was then converted and extended to fit luggage and covered with a solar panel for charging all the electronics. In the front it stayed the same, there were two children's seats with security seatbelts. But because of lack of space in the trailer, children would normally sit on the bike, Iyan in front of me and Ingis strapped in her carrier on my back. It was our support vehicle, moving very slowly, we've been driving at the speed of 10-20 km/h, stopping quite often and waiting for the horses to catch up with us.

Our expedition has been a huge learning process for us. Some days we've been lucky to meet hospitable locals, who would offer us a place to camp, shower, and home-made tortas fritas. The other days we would question ourselves - is it really worth it, going through so many hardships? I can't count how many times we had a punctured tire in our motorbike and Mo had to drive 100-200 km to the nearest town because we don't have any more spare tubes. And it's not easy to find asphalt roads in Argentina...

As the months went on, it was getting hotter and hotter. The more South we were going, the more difficult it was to find water, grass, and shade on the road. Imagine not seeing a single tree for 50-100km! Rivers which were shown on the map were dried up, most exist only in the winter.

Patagonia was getting brutally hot and windy. The wind was causing our parked motorbike to fall on the side and bent the handlebar eventually. For the first time in my life, I've experienced what windburn is on my face. Also, everyday struggling to keep our equipment in place on a packhorse was tiring us out. Things were constantly sliding, no matter how we've tried to tie them. So, forget about trotting.

We didn't have a proper pack saddle with panniers, so we've been improvising with what we have. We designed and sewed a big pack saddlebag, which we've used over the Argentinian saddle on our packhorse. Then along the way, someone gifted us an Argentinian pack saddle and we decided to give it a try, even though it was very old and looked a bit dodgy. Maybe a week afterward, our packhorse started to have saddle sores. We knew something must change and the first breakthrough happened when we arrived in the small village of Rio Pico, after about 500 km on horseback.

We were 30km before Rio Pico when the rod connecting our motorbike and trailer broke. It was at the end of the day when we were looking for a place to camp. We pushed the trailer off the road and set up a camp in quite a bad place, without water or grass.

Mo had to go on a motorbike a couple of times to fetch some water from the nearest lake, so we have enough for the horses. We also carried some grains and balanced horse feed for emergencies. The next day we woke up early and the plan was for me, Iyan, and our volunteer to go with horses, while Mo and Ingis stayed with a motorbike and the trailer to wait for some help. This road had practically no traffic, so we expected that Mo will have to wait long hours. But most of the people have a pickup truck, so once there will be someone passing by, it shouldn't be a problem to load our trailer on top of it.

30km for the horses was a whole day ride and having Iyan was slowing us down even more. Rhythmical horse movement was making Iyan sleepy after a while and then his whole body weight rests on your one hand as you still have to hold the reins with the other hand. After about 2 hours on horseback, we see a car passing by with our trailer on top of it. The car was driving very fast and didn't stop to say anything to us. But I thought it's good that Mo finally found someone to help him.

A few minutes after, Mo arrived on the motorbike with Ingis and asked if we saw a car with our trailer on it. The guy, after loading our trailer, just drove off in a rush, without consulting with Mo where to take it, what to do or where they'll meet. It looked like we were being robbed… Mo quickly left Ingis with us and went chasing the car. The road was made of loose gravel and stones, so driving a motorbike at high speed was extremely dangerous. It was a terrifying moment for me, not only thinking if Mo is going to hurt himself, but also having a perspective of losing all our belongings.

Everything was in that trailer: money, electronics, passports. Fortunately, the road didn't split anywhere, it was leading straight to Rio Pico. Mo contacted the police and started searching the streets, asking people around. He found the driver in one of the streets and you know what, he was insulted that Mo was accusing him of robbery. He said he was going to take it to the mechanic. Yeah right, hardly believable. We found a welder and took the trailer to him. We set up camp in free municipal camping which was filled with grass and began to think about changes.

The welder had for sale a single axle car trailer, just an empty base. We wanted to build on top of that a horse carriage. That way we wouldn't have to use a packhorse anymore, we would have some shelter from the sun and wind, which was especially important for the kids. We would use one horse for pulling it and we could still have 2 riding horses. Sounds like a good plan, right?

We asked the welder to build on top of that trailer a metal frame, which we would cover with some canvas. Then he made metal rods where the horse was supposed to be attached and a little storage underneath a wooden floor. It all took about a week of work and cost around £600. It wasn't exactly a pretty gypsy horse wagon which I had in mind, but it was a start.

Another challenge we were facing is how to get a harness for the horse. Neither here in Rio Pico nor in the next larger town 100 km further, did they have something even close to what we could use as a harness. And to be honest, no matter how far we look, we may not be able to find it, as that's not something people use here. There was a harness available online, but we would have to ask some Argentinian to buy it for us and wait at least another week before it arrives. We decided to do it once we reach the next town and for now, we'll build our harness using girths and leather straps.

When everything was ready, we were all very excited about our new home, we decided to try it out using the calmest of all our horses - Pomelo. Pomelo was a big horse in comparison to small Argentinian Criollos, steady and calm, honestly, nothing would scare him or bother. He was a perfect road horse, there could be a huge truck driving full speed in his direction, making our other horse go crazy, but he never showed any fear. I was letting Iyan ride him alone and I had confidence that nothing would happen. So Pomelo seemed like a perfect choice for pulling our new home.

There were four of us trying to hitch Pomelo to a cart, he was very nervous from the beginning. Slowly, we managed to do a few steps walking with him in the campsite and then the back of the carriage slightly hit some wooden post. Pomelo was out of control, he spooked and started running crazily around the campsite with the carriage flying behind him. We were afraid that a cart might be too heavy to pull, but it was barely touching the ground with Pomelo in a full gallop. Pomelo didn't stop until the carriage was destroyed.

It wasn't worth it to try picking up the pieces to rebuild it. All the metal had been broken, the wooden floor was ready to fuel the fire, even the main axle with wheels had bent in two different directions. And how the horse managed to get out of this without a single scratch on him, I don't know to this day. We didn't know whether to cry or laugh. All the hard work, all the money and time, all the hope invested in creating our new home, was destroyed in just a few seconds. It was a truly devastating moment, putting a question mark on the whole expedition. We were back to square one.

We had too much determination to give up so quickly. We abandoned leftover pieces of our carriage in the campsite, notifying some locals that they were free to sell or use it if they liked. Just like before with a packhorse and motorbike, we continued the struggle against the sun, wind, and other harsh weather conditions. The views were always stunning though, Patagonia is truly one of the most beautiful places on Earth.

We had to get to the next town, where we planned to give our horses a long break and think about what and how to do the next part of the journey. The average distance between villages is 100km, which was a 4-5 days ride for us.

Just when we approached the town of Gobernador Costa, a big truck stopped, the driver came out and gave me some fruits, sweets, and juice for the kids. He said that all this land I can see on my left and right belongs to him and if we need any help, to ask in the city for his name. That's how we met one of the most important people in our expedition. And we needed help, so when we arrived at Gobernador Costa, we asked around who is the owner of the vast land 15 km before the town.

We were pointed to Dario, he was a wealthy person, who owned few trucks, hundreds of cattle, horses, and land. Despite being rich, he was one of the most honest and helpful Argentinians we've met. We decided to leave our horses for a month to rest, hoping it would help our packhorse to recover from a saddle sore. They had a huge field to graze on. We left all our belongings in Dario's warehouse and packed only two backpacks to take with us.

We dropped the idea of continuing to El Calafate on horseback and decided to go North. We weren't prepared to cross 1,000 km of Patagonian Desert and it wasn't worth it to torture us and the horses. But we still wanted to see the South of Argentina, so we used this month's break for exploring the country as backpackers.

After a month, we came back, looking forward to meeting our horses. We hoped they were still where we left them, that no one stole them and that they hadn't run away. We could see them from far away, grazing peacefully with a herd of cows. Now, we just had to catch them… Honestly, if someone would have told me before that I'm going to spend a week catching my horses, I would laugh. The land was enormous, from the entrance gate you couldn't see the end of it in any direction. Some parts were muddy and flooded with water, giving us even more of a disadvantage.

Our horses weren't stupid, once they saw us coming with ropes the first time, they knew it's the end of their freedom. Led by mischievous Malu, who was their Alfa, he wouldn't allow them to be caught. No incentive could convince them to stop running. We tried to corner them and separate a piece of land with ropes, a few times we were so close that we could almost touch them. Again, they would break through and Malu would make everyone run to the other side of the field.

After two days of failed attempts chasing them on foot, we knew we needed help. We asked Gauchos from a nearby ranch if they could come on horseback and help us. They said they would in their free time, however, that never happened. We asked Dario for help and he sent his employees on horseback. Four Gauchos and five dogs managed to chase our horses into a corral where we could catch them. But that wasn't the end of our trouble, then we found out that Malu's back instead of getting better, had gotten worse.

Before we left him there was just a little swelling and now there's an open wound on his withers. He must have rubbed it against something or opened the skin while rolling. We couldn't use him anymore. Temporarily we had to use Pomelo as our packhorse. Malu was just following freely and Sinn was ridden. The plan was to get to the next town, 60km away, and try to sell Malu or exchange him for a different horse. As it usually happens, when one thing goes wrong, everything else starts falling apart.

About 5 km before the next town, Tecka, we had an accident where Pomelo cut his back leg. It was a really stupid accident, which could easily have been avoided and it's all our fault. You know the moment when you feel like you know your horses so well and you start neglecting basic safety? That's what happened.

Mo was bringing water for the horses from the town, as there was nothing along the road. We tied Pomelo and Malu who were tied together to a road sign and we gave water to Sinn first. They were so thirsty! But when Pomelo saw the water he started pulling. He pulled so hard that a road sign came out of the ground. That spooked both of the horses who were tied to it and they started running, dragging the sign behind them. And that's what cut Pomelo's leg. He was bleeding, but we managed to walk slowly with him these few kilometers to the town.

We were lucky to find again a free place to stay for us and the horses. We just had a long break and we'll have to take another one again. Well, that's life, never-ending problems, what can you do? You can give up and go back home or you can keep pushing forward. The good news is that we managed to sell Malu, not for a good price, but for a horse you can't use straight away we couldn't expect much.

Pomelo was put in a stable to restrict his movements, while Sinn was running free in the field. We paid the neighbor to take care of our horses and decided to go to Chile and buy a van. Why Chile? First of all, the vehicles are much cheaper than in Argentina, but still expensive if you're comparing to Europe or the US. Secondly, in Argentina as a foreigner without an Argentinian ID, you can't buy anything in your name. In Chile it's possible and the paperwork process is not so complicated. Even the motorbike wasn't bought in our name, but on paper, it belonged to our Argentinian friend. What we've been through when we bought a van in Chile is a long and separate story itself. Without going into details, let me just say that we bought a Chinese van Hafei, which was the only thing we could afford. It broke down the day we signed the paperwork, even though it was checked before by three different mechanics. We spent twice what it was worth on all the repairs.

After a month we came back to Argentina and were ready to continue the expedition. It was a breakthrough point, having a van as a support vehicle made everything easier. It wasn't big, but we made a bed in the back, some storage space underneath, and the front seats were fully loaded as well. Most importantly we had some closed space for the children to stay in case we were surprised by bad weather.

Over the past 5 months, we've spent almost every single night sleeping in a tent. It was very comfortable and spacious. We laid down all saddle pads and sheepskin on the floor had a warm sleeping bag and all our clothes served as a pillow. The children liked our little house too and had a deep and peaceful sleep in a tent. Probably only three times we've experienced pouring rain and had to keep the kids inside the tent the whole day. It's not easy to occupy them in such a tiny space, but then again they're spending entire days outdoors. So, camping with children is not difficult, as long as you remember that cooking on fire takes much longer than using gas or electricity.

When it comes to food, we needed good planning. Kids get hungry quickly and more often than adults. Preparing a fire pit and collecting firewood was one of the first things to do after setting up camp. Practically everywhere we were able to find some wood, even in the desert.

Back to the story, we're in Tecka with our new van, Pomelo's leg is cured and we're thinking what to do with our motorbike. We can't leave it behind, definitely not here in Tecka.

The neighbor who was taking care of our horses, told us, that when we were gone, someone tried to steal the bike twice. He heard a noise at night and he went out in time to scare off the thieves. But during the second attempt, he got stabbed with a knife in his chest. He showed us a little scar, we couldn't tell if it was fresh or an old scar.

We didn't know what to think about all of it, how much of the story was true. Maybe the guy just wants us to pay him more money because he protected our motorbike. It wouldn't be the first time when people lied and tried to take advantage of us. But we did feel sorry for him and so we left him lots of things which we didn't want to carry anymore that he could use or sell. Argentina seemed a pretty safe place for us, we never had a situation in which we had to fear for our life.

In the end, we exchanged our motorbike for a new horse. Dario, who we met in Gobernador Costa, had a horse for sale. It was very expensive, so we didn't even consider it before. But Dario was interested in our motorbike, so we made a deal. Contramano, our new horse, came to us loaded on top of a garbage truck. It was such a calm and well-behaved animal, I hadn't seen anything quite like him. He was beautiful, gentle, and docile, but not the smartest one though. Having spent his whole life in a stable, he was quite sensitive and required special care. We weren't sure how he'd deal with the hardships of this journey. Having three horses allowed us to rotate them in terms of riding, so no one would get too tired. Plus, we only were traveling 25-30 km per day, taking breaks every time, we reached the next village.

As we continued our journey with the new system, finally everything was falling into place. Having more space and opportunities we were also able to accept two volunteers at the same time. We would divide into two teams: a riding team and a support team.

In the early morning I leave with the horses and one of our volunteers, then when the kids were awake and had breakfast, Mo and the second volunteer would catch up with us. If everything was okay, then Mo would continue with a van forward, until he could find a good spot for a lunch break. He would start cooking, so by the time I arrive with the horses, the food would be ready. Then we take about a three hours lunch break, depending on how good the grass is, and in the afternoon we would swap.

The riding team from the morning would be a support team now, responsible for finding a good spot for the night and setting up camp. We were finding it as a good balance, spending only half a day in the saddle. We didn't get too tired and we shared responsibilities equally.

Our family has grown bigger as we got a dog, Roko, a German shepherd/Labrador mix, who was raised in the city. At first, he was scared of the horses. With time he learned to run alongside the horses and became my daughter's best friend. This dog has an unbelievable amount of patience. Ingis can ride him like a horse, pull his collar or tail and he wouldn't make a single complaint. When he has had enough of the kids for the day, he quietly walks away and hides.

So, we've had a couple of quiet weeks, where nobody was getting hurt, we didn't have any big problems and things were going smoothly. Then, we had a really long stretch of road without any villages in between. In the previous village, we weren't able to stock up much, as for vegetables they only had a couple of potatoes and rotten onions. So, we've been low on food.

One day as the road was splitting, we decided to take a little detour with our van, we've heard there's a village 30 km away. I stayed at the camp with horses and kids, Mo was trying to reach that village. 30km on a bad dirt road with our van would take about 2 hours. What wasn't shown on a map is that after 15km there's a river running through the road. No, there wasn't any bridge. If you had a high clearance 4x4 it wouldn't be a problem to cross it, but with our Chinese van, it was not possible.

While approaching the river there was a ridge which Mo didn't notice and hit it with our van. When he came back, I could sense a strong smell of petrol. Our petrol tank had gotten punctured. Wonderful. We are only 100 km away from the next town, where we can fix it, with almost no food. We had only one spare petrol can, so we tried to collect as much lost petrol in a bucket as we could.

The next morning, Mo with one of our volunteers, packed everything that they needed to survive three days and left with horses heading towards Bariloche. The kids and I and the other volunteer, had a crazy, bumpy ride to reach civilization before the petrol finished. Sticking Epoxy on at the crack wouldn't help as it was too oily. I've tried to slow down the leaking with duct tape.

We made it to the mechanic, after waiting a fair amount of time for their siesta to finish, he told me to go to the supermarket and buy "dulce de membrillo." I wasn't sure whether he's joking or not, he wants me to go and buy him some jam? Dulce de membrillo is a quince jelly and the mechanic wasn't planning to eat it. He got under our van, put some of this jelly on the petrol tank crack and you know what, it stopped leaking! I looked at him shocked asking, "So what, that's it? You're not gonna do anything else?"

According to him, "It's gonna hold on forever." I wish he was right. It did hold on… for two days. And then, again I smelled petrol. Eventually, we got it welded with a different mechanic.

Mo with the horses came after two days, making 55 km on the second day, which is our biggest distance done in one day. He was rushing to go to the hospital, as his foot got infected and swollen. He keeps walking barefoot around the camp and a few days ago a horse accidentally stepped on his foot. That wound got infected and he couldn't walk anymore. But that was the least of our problems…

Bariloche is a very significant place in our journey, it's where we started and where we finished the first season of our expedition. We bought Sinn and Malu in Bariloche and after doing 1,000 km on horseback we came back to this town and had to stop our journey. What an irony. But let me tell you what actually happened.

It was very difficult to find a place to stay with horses here. Nobody had grass and nobody was willing to share it if they did. Bariloche, being a big touristy place, has a lot of horse-riding centers around. Lots of competition means little grazing land. We've had some contacts from before and tried calling everyone we knew asking for a place. We had to stay a week here to fix the van and give the horses a rest.

Finally, one old acquaintance agreed to let us use his place. The deal was that we'd give him a packet of cigarettes, one bale of hay and we'd pay him for shoeing our horses. He didn't have any grass, nor water. We had to buy hay for our horses and keep them tied on short ropes the whole week. He had like 30 dogs chained around his land in different places and about 16 of his horses. Because his well was almost dry and he was struggling to water his own horses, we've been driving every day to the petrol station to fill up big water bottles for our animals.

We noticed our hay disappeared slowly every day and apparently according to the owner of this place, we agreed on one hay bale per day, not in total. As we had to leave the van with a mechanic, we couldn't go and buy more hay from the city. That meant our horses had very little to eat for a few days. And there were many other small things, because of which we wanted to leave this place as soon as possible.

He also was supposed to shoe our horses. One whole day he spent just removing old shoes from Pomelo. And a day before we planned to leave, he started shoeing the first horse. It was honestly a dreadful sight, we saw how the hooves of Sinn had cracked and chipped off. When we tried to point out to him that he shouldn't be doing it this way, he got offended, saying he grew up around horses and he knows what he's doing. He managed to put two shoes on, with Mo's help, while I was packing the van preparing for leaving.

On the roof of our van, we had a motorbike trailer, secured with slack-lines, where we stored hay and horse feed. So, I was on top of the van packing trailer, while the car started slowly moving forward. My son Iyan was playing in the front seats and Mo must have left keys in the ignition when he was moving the van. Iyan turned the ignition on and because the van was parked in the 1st gear, it started rolling. I jumped off of the rooftop and ran, only to be terrified that Iyan was still in the front, just before the van hit a tree. Thank God Ingis wasn't anywhere near when all that was happening.

Everyone was fine, but the front windshield of the van completely crashed.

Cheap Chinese piece of garbage! The problem was that we couldn't fix this in Argentina because spare parts for this make and model don't exist in this country. We would have to drive to Santiago de Chile to be able to fix it. We couldn't do that either as we would be stopped by the police if they saw the damage to the van. It wasn't a road-safe vehicle anymore. Another thing is that we couldn't afford to fix it now, as our savings were finishing and, in a month, we were planning to return to the UK to work. So, our situation was very tense and complicated, we had to leave Bariloche, but we couldn't.

After considering hundreds of different scenarios, we came to a decision. I would fly back home with the kids, Mo would take the horses and continue traveling until he finds a good place to leave them for a winter break. We found a nice guy who let us leave our broken van in his backyard. Mo found a volunteer to travel with him and with a packhorse they continued heading North. Without taking back any luggage with me, I was quickly on my way to Buenos Aires, hoping to survive a 13-hour flight back to London, alone with two kids. I don't recommend it. It can destroy your nerves. It was a day flight, so forget about the kids sleeping. I needed a week to recover after that.

Mo joined me in Europe after two weeks. He found a ranch in Villa Lago Melliquina where we could leave the horses. It wasn't cheap to pay for their stay and food for 6 months, but we didn't have time or means to find something better.

We got a job in one of the campsites on the south coast in the United Kingdom, where we worked for 6 months during the summer season. We bought a proper motorhome for a bargain price and we shipped it to Argentina. In October 2019 we came back to continue our journey. However, this time we were much more prepared.

Having learned through our mistakes the last season, everything was much more organized now. We had an unbelievable amount of storage in the vehicle. We've added a big black crate on the back, which was used mostly for carrying hay. We've cut open the sides behind the back wheels and used space underneath the van for storage as well. With a proper kitchen, bathroom, and two bedrooms it feels like a high life now. Our horses survived winter but lost weight. It was amazing to reunite with them after so long.

Ever since we began our trek again, we keep going North, staying close to the Andes mountains. There are still lots of challenges, but we have more time to enjoy the horseback journey itself now. Our horses are amazing and would go anywhere with us. Each one is different and special in its own way. We trust them and we love them. Maybe we're crossing Argentina so slowly because we know that in the end, we'll have to sell them. We're not in any rush, we take time to enjoy the little things.

Since July 2018, when we began our trip, we only did 2,000 km so far and still have another 2,000 km more to go. We found a good system. We can be quite independent in harsh terrain, carry enough food and water for us and the horses.

Most importantly, the kids have their little space to play, shelter from the burning sun, some toys, and books. Until they're big enough to ride and control the horses by themselves, we'll have to continue the journey with the support of a vehicle. But eventually, it's our goal to travel purely on horseback as a family, living a simple life out in nature. Discovering the world as people used to do it hundreds of years ago.

Bucking the Trend

BY EMMA ANDERSON

A few hours north-east of San Martin de Los Andes, Argentina, there is a beautiful Estancia which will always have a special place in my heart. It's where I fell in love with adventure travel by horseback. From London Heathrow, it's a two-day journey to reach the Estancia. Via Madrid and Buenos Aires, a quick dash across the city to the domestic airport, then jump on board a propeller plane which flies precariously between two mountain peaks for a bumpy landing at San Martin, which is more or less a wooden cabin.

A few hours by truck and finally, you have arrived. The Estancia is about 15,000 hectares, that's approximately 150 square km. I was a teenager the first time I visited with my family and I was on a ranch which is equivalent in size to half of the Isle of Wight - a fifth of New York City.

The Estancia is a working ranch and therefore your daily or multi-day ride usually has a purpose, often to move cattle. Each day you would wake up, tack up, and follow Argentine gauchos to explore the vast wilderness. Ancient hill-top burial sites, hidden caves, and snow-topped volcanoes, all in a day's ride.

One evening we rode high up on a mountain, leaving our horses once the rock turned to scree, and climbed on foot the rest of the way to a cliff-top. From here we watched the world's largest flying bird, the Andean Condor with a 10ft wingspan, drop from their perch and fly into the sunset. It would be typical to ride for 7 to 9 hours each day, breaking in the afternoon at a sheltered spot where an asado has been slowly barbecuing for hours. Your lunch is served; a mouth-watering and tender beef rib served on a plate of crusty bread and an ice-cold Quilmes—a perfect time to grab the sheepskin from your saddle and siesta.

If you are a fan of horse riding in a wild country, Patagonia is the place for you—it's an adventure riding Mecca. Entire days spent riding through endless grasslands and sleeping under the stars. I had never experienced space like this before. Countless stars light up the sky even in the darkest of nights. No head torch is required to make a midnight dash for a wild wee! No skyscrapers or streetlights to obscure the horizon or block out the stars, no boundaries or fences to halt your gallop, you stop when your horse decides to.

The Criollo horses are stunning and tough and nothing seems to faze them. Rein them towards a steep bank or after a runaway calf and they'll fire you towards it with such strength, agility and speed, your brain will catch up a few moments later.

The saddles are made up of thick woolen and foam pads, the saddle tree and sheepskin lashed together. It's like riding in a woolly armchair and when taken apart, makes for a surprisingly comfortable bed. You could be sleeping on them for nights at a time, under a tent or tarp if need be. Waking one morning, we noticed fresh tracks of something circling where a few of us had slept—a puma had come in for a closer look.

This is where I came to grips with the concept of "clean dirt." By the end of the day, my face would be black with earth and dust, not fumes or pollution from the London Underground. Camps would be set up near glacial streams, and a freezing stream makes for a great shower and spa treatment (so long as you stay upstream of the cattle). Besides, everyone else is just as dirty as you are. Although come to think of it, maybe that's why the puma left us in peace.

On one particular camping trip, we spent four days riding through the rolling Patagonia steppe passing armadillos, guanacos, rutting stags, and wild boar… but not one single person or road. We arrived at an Indian Reservation which was home to the family of one of the gauchos. Here we met his mother who invited us in for a cup of maté (tea). Her home was small and earthly. A wooden lean-to propped up against one walled room with sparse furniture and a clay-oven. I naively thought how unfortunate she was to have so little. But the way she glowed when she talked about her family and her home, it was clear she was rich in love and happiness.

I was hooked. I developed an absolute thirst for adventure. I wanted to explore the world, to ride across the wild country, and experience other horse cultures. My eldest sister, Sarah, went on to spend two seasons working at the same estancia. This became a fantastic excuse for the rest of us to go back and visit her… a few times! Not only was I about to commit to an awesome and rather expensive hobby of world-travel, but I also returned home with a completely different outlook on life. My material possessions and dramatic "friendships," which had been so important before, now were less so. My values had changed. I wasn't the center of the universe anymore. I was a part of it, sharing the world with many different people from different walks of life.

For me, this trip was transformational. I decided to pursue a career that meant I could keep traveling and help others to have similar experiences. This trip inspired me to become an experienced rider, wilderness guide, and expedition leader and I continue to work in adventure travel some fifteen years later.

During those long rides in Patagonia, I started to map out the next few years. I was trying to solve a problem, how could I keep traveling and do the things I was meant to do like go to university and start my career. How could I do both?

Despite what teachers and other people said, I wasn't sure that university was the right path for me. But growing up in the UK Home Counties, this is "what you did." It was expected of you to go to school to get good GCSEs and A-Levels, go on to university to get a good degree, get a job, and finally "settle down." Of course, I understood the benefits a degree would bring and that by having such supportive parents, I was privileged to have the opportunity to go. Although, it was a time of recession in the UK and I thought perhaps holding down a job might look better on my CV. I needed more time to make an almost thirty-thousand-pound decision.

I always say I do my best thinking from the saddle, so I decided to take a year to be sure I was making the right decision. I spent this year traveling and riding through Australia, New Zealand, and the United States with my sister, Naomi, who had coincidentally just finished her degree. Whilst I was working double shifts and trying to save for our big adventure, I noticed that people were beginning to question my choices. If I didn't get a degree, how else did I expect to get a job? If I went traveling, are mom and dad paying for it? I felt like I was beginning to stray from what society expected me to do, and society was letting me know what they thought about it.

It was around this time that I came up with an analogy which was has stuck with me over the years. I pictured a shoal of salmon swimming downstream. Suddenly, instinct kicked in and one of the salmon turns to swim upstream, against the current. The other fish looked and wondered what the salmon was doing. Some might keep on swimming; others may turn to swim upstream too. I felt like I was that salmon, turning against the current of what society expected and following my own path. I told myself, it's okay to be the salmon.

Who hasn't watched "The Horse Whisperer" and imagined themselves wearing chaps and a cowboy hat, on a chestnut quarter horse roping cattle? I love this film (but equally can't watch it without a box of tissues). A few notes of the soundtrack or the horses running in slow motion and I'm gone. I'm not crying, you're crying!

Working on a ranch in the United States became my next dream. After a few weeks of searching online and a few dozen more emails (most of which were left unanswered), I found a guest ranch in Montana that agreed for me to go out and "work" as an intern for their summer season. Can I point out here that when I say "work," I mean, "volunteer." Of course, you do actually work, usually from 5 am until the guests go to bed, but this is not paid, it's for the experience.

So, I applied for a visa, packed a bag, and set off to the other side of the world… alone. I was still a novice traveler. I remember my flight was delayed and I missed my connection in Utah. I stayed overnight in an airport hotel and this was the first meal I had eaten alone in a restaurant. Boy was I on a real adventure now.

The ranch in Montana is sandwiched perfectly between Yellowstone National Park to the south, and the Rocky Mountains and the Canadian border to the north. Trail rides would wind through green pastures and wildflower meadows, pass remnants of long-gone homesteads, splash through bubbling creeks and climb over mountain passes. Their almost 100-head herd was a mixed bunch; mostly American Quarter horses and Mustangs, but also Connemara's, Percherons, and Belgian Draughts. Montana was all I had hoped for. I had arrived in Big Sky Country.

Guests would visit the family-run ranch for a week and take part in a range of activities including trail rides, barrel racing, cattle cuttin' and roping, cook-outs, and campfire singalongs. The main focus of the ranch though is natural horsemanship. Guests would learn how to work together in partnership with their horse, using methods from Pat Parelli and Buck Brannaman (the real "Horse Whisperer").

As an intern, your role is effectively a ranch hand so you help out on the ranch and look after both the horses and the guests. Depending on your level of experience, you would also be assigned a few colts to bring on and help train throughout the season. I was learning about natural horsemanship for the first time and in all honesty, hadn't given that much deep thought to a horse's personality before. During the first trail ride I assisted, I rode up next to the main guide and quietly asked if there was anything specific I should be doing. She said no, she was checking my riding ability and the "horse would tell her what kind of rider I was." No pressure then.

I seemed to pass the test and was later assigned a beautiful dark bay mare, Zera. She had been backed and was going through early training as a youngster when she had unfortunately broken her stifle. Once she had recovered, she was turned out to pasture for a few years and was now fit to be brought on as a guest horse. She was fast, fiery, and full of attitude (I quickly fell for her). She was an absolute handful and challenged me constantly.

At the beginning of our partnership, I'd be out leading a trail ride and suddenly lose both steering and breaks. Once I learned more of the horsemanship techniques, or "horse-wo-manship," we soon gained respect for one another and she came on beautifully. Such was our level of trust that on one of the longer trail rides, I couldn't remember in which direction stood a gate that led home. I rode along, trying to jolt my memory and consequently avoid several hours of back-tracking. In the end, I decided to drop my reins and ask the expert. Thankfully, Zera led us home.

Lots of the riding and horsemanship games on the ranch were done bareback. Riding bareback literally brings you closer to the horse and helps to improve your balance, strength, and posture. Another test when first I arrived at the ranch had been to assist a full trail ride bareback. Bringing the herd in each morning, also bareback, was my favorite time of day. The horses that weren't chosen for the guests or training were turned out to graze and the rest would be let out to join them at the end of the day. So in the morning, three of us interns would head out in the pick-up to find the herd and bring them in again.

Once we had tracked the herd down, two of us would jump out armed with only rope head collars and a lead rein. One of us would pick a lead mare and start riding towards home, the other would pick a reliable horse to push the herd on from the rear and pick up any stragglers. It was important to bring the entire herd in so they could be regularly checked over. If some were missing it could mean they were sick or injured, their home was also shared by bears and rattlesnakes.

Horses have an incredible herd instinct and when a herd of almost 100 horses are racing for home, staying in control of the one you are on can be quite the challenge. Depending on the horse you've picked, and what mood they are in that day, you might be able to stay in control. Otherwise, their instinct to charge after the herd would win and you would just have to give up, go with it, and not fall off. It is their instinct after all. I needed enough grip to keep me on at a flat out-gallop over rough terrain, jumping the odd ditch and ducking under low branches, whilst not squeezing the horse on into a faster pace. This was one hell of a rush and my heart is racing now just thinking about it.

I didn't realize how much my riding was improving until a while later. Naomi had come out to the ranch and she went out to bring the herd in one morning. I got up a bit later and walked down with the guests to watch the herd run into the corral. This is an incredible moment to witness: watching the sunrise over the valley whilst hearing the thundering of hooves gradually approaching.

On this particular morning, a speckled-grey mare that we often picked to bring up the rear loped into the coral wearing a rope head collar and lead rein – and with no rider. It was one of those horrendous moments when your insides turn to ice and my stomach just about fell out of my ass.

I jumped off the fencepost and vaulted onto that horse with athleticism I'll never have again without adrenaline. The next minute, I was flying down the tree-line and searching for my sister, my mind racing through different scenarios. A kilometer later, I saw another intern emerge from the trees. Disheveled and dirty, but luckily no more injured than a bruised ego. Relieved, she climbed on behind me and we walked back to the ranch where Naomi stood waving… this time she'd driven the truck back instead.

Looking back on it, what I learned out in Montana vastly improved not only my riding ability and confidence but also my understanding of horses. Plus, I came away with a serious set of biceps from lifting western saddles weighing up to 60lbs.

I learned how to read the physical and mental health of each horse. A horse will often tell you what it needs. If a "bomb-proof" guest horse uncharacteristically showed signs of anxiety, naughty behaviors, or ignored cues from a rider, we'd listen and respond. It might be the horse needed a skill refresher having had a lot of beginner riders. It would be common for beginner riders to ask for multiple responses from their mount, for example, kicking a horse on and then immediately and nervously pulling on the reins. Naturally, this is confusing and frustrating for both horse and rider and both likely need a brief skill refresher! Or maybe, the horse just needed time to be a horse again.

We'd let them out for a mini-break in their pasture or take them for a free ride in whichever direction and at whatever pace they wanted - something to blow the butterflies away.

By this time, I was living with considerable back pain. I have been bitten, kicked, thrown off, stepped on, and somehow even head-butted by horses, but a particularly bad fall in Argentina had left part of my spine fractured. It happened when I was mounting a young horse and before I could swing into the saddle, it took off like a bucking bronco. I think I lasted about 8 seconds (maybe I should consider a career in the rodeo...) before I was unceremoniously dumped onto a pile of rocks (... maybe not).

When the pain didn't subside back home, I went to see my doctor who pinned it as "growing pains." Not until five years later did a scan finally reveal my crumpled coccyx which bent, almost at a right-angle inward.

This injury causes referral pain in my lower back, hips, and shoulders, and one of my legs is actually over an inch shorter than the other. In a random coincidence, it turned out that Zera had one hind leg shorter than the other following her stifle injury. This was on the opposite side to mine so bizarrely we 'evened each other out' and when riding her I felt no pain. My pain is now manageable so long as I diligently practice things like physio and Pilates. Besides, a doctor once told me on an expedition in China that my coccyx will likely be "straightened out" through childbirth... so there is that to look forward to.

Needless to say, I came up against a few challenges in my attempts to keep going on adventures. Over the next few years, I'd have to re-build savings, quit jobs, and end relationships. None of these turned out to be bad things. But I found that an even bigger challenge in pursuing adventure was finding the confidence to stand up for my decisions when society questioned them.

As I mentioned, the society I lived in had certain expectations of you: go to college, get a job, buy a house, get married, and have kids. Let me be clear, I am not saying there is anything wrong with wanting any of these things. Everyone should have the right to choose their own path. But what I found is that when choosing mine, when my thirst for adventure seemed to be taking me down a different route than what was expected, sooner or later, people started to question my choices. My particular favorite was "don't you think you should get a real job?" Others included (and are not limited to): How can you afford to go off on a jolly like that? What are you going to do when you come back to reality? Aren't you just putting it off? These questions may seem innocent enough, but I found them laced with judgment. Suddenly I found that other people, who may or may not know me, were voicing their unsolicited opinions of how I should live my life. One woman I met when I was guiding actually advised me to go and work on luxury yachts, "they're always hiring and you're pretty enough." Wow.

Perhaps sometimes people are correct, maybe a dream will fail, but isn't it from failure when we learn most? Questioning someone's choices in this way can have a detrimental effect. By questioning rather than supporting, it could be enough for them to give up before they're even out of the starting gate. Dreams are incredibly personal, and in many ways, fragile. They need to be given room to grow.

I came to think that these people were simply projecting. When they hear your idea, they imagine themselves in your or your parents' shoes and devise their own view based on how they would feel doing it. Their personal opinion or fear is then projected onto you. Once I realized this, I found it much easier to answer their questions with confidence. I remembered that it's okay to be the salmon. My answer and mantra became I Can and I Will, Watch Me.

Of course, I also had "real jobs." After I did finish my degree, I worked in the events and adventure travel industries and led international trekking challenges. Anyone who has also worked in these industries will know that it comes with long and unsociable hours. After a few years of organizing overseas expeditions, I felt like my hard work was being taken advantage of rather than valued. Some people seemed to think this was par for the course. A "like it or lump it" attitude was deeply rooted in the company. I thought it was about time for my next adventure. I quit my job and set off to work as a trail guide on a wilderness outfitter in Alberta, Canada.

I'm sure you'll be surprised to hear that there were people who again questioned me. Why was I leaving a good position, it was something I had worked hard for? It was true that I was leaving a good opportunity and unfinished qualifications behind. I asked for advice from those closest to me, my family, as I always do. By now they of course knew I would have my reasons and encouraged me to go for it, to follow my dreams. They understood dreams need space to grow. I could see that the main questions were coming from someone I was dating at the time; he was controlling and didn't want me to go. Fortunately, my Mantra kicked in.

Canada was by far the most challenging riding I have ever done. The outfitter was located in the Kananaskis Mountains, not far from Banff

National Park, and home to moose, bears, and wolves. They offered shorter trail rides from the ranch and multi-day pack trips into the mountains. As it drifted into winter and the leaves turned to yellow, the elk hunting season opened and we also crewed on regular drop-camp trips. This involved leading a group of hunters to a specific location in the mountains, dropping off their camp, and riding back out with their horses in tow. A week or so later we would return to collect them. To get to these camps you need to cover seriously rough terrain; it is not for the faint-hearted. To give you an idea of the type of country, this is where "The Revenant" was filmed.

Not all of the trips went smoothly and a mix up occurred on one. We had mounted at the road ahead and set off quickly into the forestry for we had a lot of ground to cover. After an hour or so we reached the edge of the tree line and a wide rider came into view.

We picked out a path alongside it and followed the river as it snaked along the valley and into the mountains. The mountains seemed to loom over us and eventually, we reached the base of one which the hunters knew led to their favorite spot to camp. I looked up at the ground ahead where a steep slope of mud gave way to boulders and dense forestry.

"We can't go up there,'' I thought. Sure enough, the hunters reassured us that this was the correct way and so we began to climb.

After a lot of slipping, panting, and coaxing of the pack horses, we reached the top and followed a sharp ridge-line for at least another hour. Finally, we reached a clearing where the hunters could point out our destination, their camping spot. Unfortunately, they were pointing to a beautiful meadow on the mountain next to the one that we were currently stood. With no way across, doubling back was our only option.

I'm afraid of heights and I'll never forget the sheerness of some of the slopes which we now had to tackle at speed as we were losing the daylight. At times I felt like I was leaning so far back in my saddle to balance my horse that I would topple out the back door. I felt like I was recreating the famous scene in "The Man from Snowy River."

It certainly proved to be a challenging day, navigating our way hundreds of feet high in the mountains while leading a train of 2-3 horses each behind us. In those moments you have to hold your nerve and put pure trust and blind faith in your horse. Luckily, they were extremely well trained and hardened to the mountains which they roamed and of course when the going got too rough, we walked beside them.

At last, the wilderness spat out me and my trusty appaloosa at the road head after dark. My Stetson had new scratches, bits of twigs and leaves were sticking out from everywhere and I was grinning from ear to ear. Surviving that ride felt like my biggest achievement since graduating! With all the extra grain and carrots I sneaked him, my appaloosa was chuffed too.

Alberta enforces strict hunting regulations and only at certain times of year may you hunt a particular number of animals, depending on many environmental factors including their current population. This year proved to be an unusual elk hunting season in that the elk remained elusive to the hunters. There were too many predators around.

One day, the boss radioed us at the ranch to go and re-supply his static camp. Unlike the drop-camps, these had a more luxurious set up with their cook teams and each canvas tent came equipped with camp beds, furs, and wood stoves.

A friend of mine drove the wagon carrying new supplies to the camp, while I followed on a fresh horse which was to be swapped out with one of the hunter's horses.

Arriving at the camp, I saw to the horses and visited the cook team who relayed to me events of the last few restless nights. A pack of wolves had been in the camp overnight, they had left fresh tracks behind the tents and were perhaps scared off by the dogs. Grizzly and black bears had also been spotted, daily, in the vicinity of the camp. Bear and wolf hide now hung from trees in camp.

I learned in Canada not only to trust your horse but also to listen to it. If it stops dead in its tracks, ears pricked, nostrils snorting; maybe there is something out there in the dense forestry that your mere human senses can't yet pick up. This did happen on more than one occasion when there were grizzlies around.

This sort of environment makes for tough people. It was a very male-dominated mountain culture. It wasn't enough to just be a good rider. To be tough enough for the elements, you had to be "mountain tough." Like, if you weren't born to a wolf pack you weren't part of the club. Whilst the crew was made up mostly of women, after a particularly hard day of fixing neighboring ranchers' fencing and clearing their fields, only the male crew members were offered a thank you.

I felt that I was only really seen as an equal midway through the season. Hard work, continuing to work while injured, and being able to hold your beer seemed to do the trick.

I love working as a guide and meeting people from all over the world. With hours to pass while in the saddle you can sit and enjoy the view, share stories with guests, hear about their ambitions in life, make cross-continental friendships, and find inspiration for the next adventure. When you're riding, you are usually looking ahead at the horizon rather than directly into the eyes of the person you are talking to, the same as hiking. This makes it easier to open up and perhaps share something troubling you.

As a guide, people often confide their troubles and tragedies to me. This was their healing; spending days connecting with their horses, testing themselves in a new and wild environment, and pushing themselves beyond their comfort zones. They needed someone who wasn't from 'home' to listen. I was a safe place to share as after all, they are unlikely to see me again. In this way, I have found riding to be very therapeutic. The physical act of moving forwards is a positive and cathartic one.

When you are in a wild country, away from pressures of work and bills, and far removed from bosses, colleagues, and (forgive me) partners and children, you have an opportunity to re-connect with your true self. You have a chance to take a breath and remember what's important to you.

In the travel industry, this is often referred to as "escapism." I don't care for this phrase because to me, it suggests you are running away from your problems. Instead, I like to think of it as "presentism." It's finding the time to step aside from the hectic, fast-paced lifestyle in which we find ourselves where we put our heads down to forge onwards; often just surviving, not thriving.

How many times have you come home from work, exhausted, your partner asks how your day was and you respond with, "I got through it." Take a breather. Be present. With our heads down, we're missing the view.

If you can, find time for yourself to step away and be present in the moment. For me, I am truly present when on horseback, preferably in the wilderness, experiencing a new and exciting horse culture. But these moments can also be closer to home. Take up painting. Go for a wild swim. Climb a tree. Walk a long-distance trail in your area. Whatever it is, take the time to re-connect with yourself (although if you have the money to go and book a luxury riding safari, I would!). Yes, you might have to conquer a fear to make this happen. You might have to say no to someone, cancel plans, or push back a deadline. You might be afraid of what people will say, of being questioned. The only important question is ''will it make you happy?'' If so, go for it.

Having the confidence to buck the trend and follow my path is something I'll always be proud of. It's led me to some pretty crazy places. When my sister and I backpacked across Australia and New Zealand, we stopped off at different riding establishments along the way. We herded deer on Clydesdale Thoroughbred X's and took a 14hr bus into the outback to get polo-crosse ponies fit for the tournament season. It turned out that the weeks we spent living with local people like this were the best out of our 8-month trip. Our hosts took us to their favorite spots which we would never have seen on the tourist trail.

Of course, not all my plans have worked out. We were due to spend a few weeks at a station on the north island of New Zealand, helping a farmer turn his "shabby-chic" farm into riding stables. Rather than "shabby-chic," this was "shabby-shit." There were maggots in the kitchen, ponies too lame to be ridden and the manager spent an evening watching us watch TV. Together, we decided that not all adventures need to be seen through and we moved onto bigger and better things.

Horse riding adventures have shaped my life. My next adventure will be to join the Long Riders Guild (a group of hard-as-nails explorers who have ridden over 1,000 continuous miles). When I started planning a solo and unsupported ride of my own, I turned to social media for inspiration. This had a detrimental effect. Seeing other people's pictures, already out there, riding across continents made me feel massively intimated. Do I have what it takes? I don't even have a horse. My self-esteem and creativity took a knock.

Soon enough, my feet became itchy and I am now looking to the east for my next adventure, maybe Mongolia or Kyrgyzstan. As I am also getting married next year, no doubt the questions again start to come my way soon. Won't you be newly married? When are you planning to have children? Don't wait too long. I'm not just projecting my concerns here, I was asked by a family member recently, "so you'll be giving us babies, soon right?" Lucky for me, my partner shares my passion for adventure and will no doubt see my trip as an opportunity to plan his own climbing expedition.

Bucking the trend has certainly been a challenge to overcome in pursuing my adventures and following my own path. I don't think people will ever stop projecting their opinions onto me, however, with age, it is getting easier to overlook their comments and answer their questions with confidence. Now I feel a combination of enjoyment and rebellious pride when I tell people what adventure I have dreamed up next.

Sure enough, there will be more challenges to overcome and fears to face throughout the journey. Fear of pain from my back injury, fear of being tough enough, fear of failing, fear of wildlife that can eat you are only a few examples. Putting myself directly in the path of these obstacles has taught me resilience, confidence and to be a far better rider. It has led me to many priceless, wonderful memories and shaped who I am today.

If you feel like bucking the trend too, I welcome you to borrow my mantra: I Can and I Will, Watch Me. And please remember… it's okay to be the salmon.

Going "Bush" in New Zealand

BY ANNIE HACKETT

Gidday, I'm writing as a 19-year-old Kiwi girl from the little Island of New Zealand. A lot of people confuse our flag with Australia's, some even our accents, but if you have never been to NZ, I can assure you that our unique culture and climate is well worth the visit.

My name is Annie Rose Hackett. I've been lucky enough to grow up rurally in the Far North of New Zealand, surrounded by horses, ponies, and animals of all sorts. We have always had beaches nearby, making for great adventures with my younger five siblings to ride down on horseback.

Horses for me began as a hobby when I was 5, but now in my 19th year of life, they are my life. My world has begun to revolve around anything and everything horse-related. As I got older, I began to learn more in-depth alongside my Aunty Emma with different training methods and riding styles, and over the last several years have put together a little bit of everything I have learned from many different people. Some from the "old school cowboy," a bit from my nana, and even from the crazy lady down the road who set me to work as a 15-year-old backing Clydesdales.

Finally, after the Winter of 2016 had passed, my aunty and I spontaneously took both our green bush ponies for a taste of the coast. 90-mile beach (which is, in fact, only 55 miles long) gave us a week I will never forget. We began our week searching for a place to set up camp on a farm bordering on the giant Te Paki sand dunes. After finding a lovely hidden corner nestled in the shelter of a pine forest, we decided to give our ponies their first taste of salt air and sandy adventures. I very quickly learned that my solid chestnut gelding Scooby had a very strong phobia of tourist busses, boogie boards, information huts, cattle stops, tourists, and probably even the giant dunes themselves!

I wasn't letting that stop me from enjoying the golden sand between my toes. Tugging at his lead we raced around all the touristy commotion with Scooby practically towing us in his panic, and found ourselves a lovely lone dune to play around and start desensitizing the ponies.

After a while of settling our feisty steeds, excitement got the better of me, so I took off again, my pony trailing behind me down a steep dune. The wind caught our manes and the sand warmed our hooves, I was in paradise, and I'm sure Scooby was too.

On a typical Christmas day in NZ, we go to the beach. The only downside is when we kids are all called up for food, it's a mad rush of red-hot feet on red hot sand, burning our way as quick as our fitness allowed to reach the coolness of the grass. Well let me tell you, I was starting to get that feeling. At the bottom of the dune, I noticed an absolutely magical oasis of crystal-clear water! We bee-lined straight towards it but before I could stop, I felt a tingly, unnatural feeling beneath my feet. It was too late. Scooby's rope tightened in my grip as I flew over the wobbly sand while he plummeted straight down underground.

Quicksand.

Grandad had ALWAYS warned my aunty and I about this. "I've seen one too many horses get lost under quicksand, Annie," he used to tell me, "It's important never to panic, or you'll panic the horse, then you're sure to never get the bugger out."

Well, I panicked. My darling pony was getting helplessly sucked into the earth and I knew I would never be strong enough to save him. As tears welled up in my eyes, I couldn't help but scream at him, "GET UP YOU EGG, C'MON SCOOBS, HUP HUP HUP, GEEEET UUUUUP."

All four of his legs were well under, and the sand was quickly lapping around his belly. The only part of him I could grab was his halter lead. Aunty Em began to position her hearty little mare, Bailey, in case we had to use her to help give Scooby some extra horsepower at his head. I couldn't even see my boy through my tears anymore, I could only make out the frantic jerking of his neck flailing around. He knew he was in serious danger.

My yanking on his halter was doing jack all, so I grabbed a nearby stick and gave him a good blow on his rump, which at this point was about knee height off the ground. To my surprise, that seemed to pump all the adrenaline he had left straight into his hindquarters, and in an attempted rear, he managed to pull his front hooves right up onto the sands shiny surface. Hope was in the air.

Bailey nickered out encouragement to him from the sideline. It was just too dangerous to bring her closer to help tow him, as our ropes were only 6ft long. After what seemed like a lifetime of screaming and whacking and hauling, (but was only really a matter of 10 seconds), I began rocking his head back and forwards until his whole body got the idea and after enough momentum had built up, he took his shot and scrambled with all his power, fighting the sand and heaving his weighed down legs gradually to the surface, up 'n out.

The four of us were trembling as nobody will hopefully ever see again. You bet we walked straight back to our bush corner, fed, watered, and high lined our ponies for the night.

Well, I supposed I did ask for an adventure. We sure did get a good wake up call to quicksand, and I personally will NEVER take the dunes for granted ever again. Nature and respect really do go hand-in-hand.

Day two and three were better. After a lot of desensitizing to the big four-axle tourist busses, we got in some lovely bareback rides over the dune ridges, (staying strictly to the top) and good gallops up the beach. Along with our typical sunny weather, we were in paradise.

That night, after finding some logs to pop over on our evening bareback ride through the farm, we high-lined the ponies as per usual, tying on their reflective fabric strips to their halters in case one got off during the night and needed to be easily found in the torchlight. Well, it wasn't just us who might need to be finding animals in the torchlight.

Three big bangs bounced off the pine trees near us and echoed into the horse float, immediately waking us both. Peeking over the back ramp we could make out big light beams flicking off into the bush. A truck revved. Some of the local cattle began stampeding together. The high-powered rifle went off again, this time closer and louder than before.

It was a Saturday night, only typical of Northland to host drunken spotlighters, with nothing better to do than poach the local cattle. Aunty Emma pulled on her gumboots and gave me our game plan, "If they get closer with that spotlight, we better turn on the car headlights to warn we are here. The reflectors on the horses will easily be noticed and could be mistaken for eyes instead of fabric from a distance. If they do come up here still with our lights on, we need to get in the car and lock ourselves in, okay?" Em was aware that we could be locked into the float from the outside.

I nodded back with confidence. We sat, waiting, watching, wondering, and wishing they would go away. After 15 cautious minutes, their engine revs faded back down the gravel road and no more shots were heard. With settled horses and settled minds, we puttered off back to our cozy pile of blankets, all huddled between the manure-splattered walls of the float.

The following day was our rest day to explore and just reflect on some of the things we had been working on with the horses. After successfully navigating over the dunes, we got to a lake. The beach had been too choppy to swim in, so we tested our waters and plunged in aboard our ponies' backs. Scooby loved it, to say the least. His big sturdy hooves which always looked out-of-proportion to his solid 14.1hh figure, made the perfect little paddles, boosting him out 20 meters into the lake, all while I was stuck on his back struggling to turn his head around and head back to where I could reach the bottom. I guess he had finally found his talent.

We realized the other side of the lake was just below our campsite. It was nearing dark and to ride back was a good hour, so as I exchanged glances with Aunty Em, we both knew we had the same idea.

Scooby could probably swim us over there, but Bailey, with her little hooves and fine conformation, would struggle to make it across the current near the other side. Alas, we gave it a shot, figuring that worst-case-scenario we just drift downstream until we hit the sand.

Scoobs powered into the lake, ears pricked to the far away pines on the other side, Bailey and Emma bringing up the rear. We boosted ahead and as we started drifting into the current, I hopped off my pony and grabbed his neck so I could float alongside him, letting him have his head. Over my shoulder, I noticed that Emma had done the same, but more to help kick along her mare, who was visibly huffing and panting, only just holding her pretty bay head above the water level.

However, as we neared the opposing bank, I realized that the 80-meter swim was the easy part and that navigating through all the fallen pines submerged under the murky surface would be more dangerous than I expected. We bounced up that bank with only some chest and leg scrapes, but Bailey was exhausted from her swim and after clambering up the bank, showed several minor puncture wounds on her shoulder and fetlock. We were too proud of our ponies to stress much—they weren't life-threatening wounds —and walked back to camp grinning from ear to ear, soaking wet, but stoked.

We continued to travel around to some of our childhood beaches and campsites in the Far North for five days, overcoming and accomplishing more and more than we ever expected to every day. A 500-meter single lane boardwalk suspended two meters high, cantering through soft deep sandy vehicle tracks (which Grandad also had warned us against, as horses could easily trip over themselves), steep cliff climbs, scary nights camping down old forestry tracks, and being discovered by a couple of wild horses roaming the forest.

The whole experience was just my first of many to come, and I didn't regret it one bit. I learned resilience, gained respect for nature, more trust in my horse than I thought possible, and the fact that we overcame most of our fears (Scooby is still slightly timid around buses and boogie boards, silly boy), but ALL of our challenges and obstacles that we faced, really felt like we could do anything. The four of us left the Far North stronger and more capable than when we arrived, all through growing a partnership with our ponies and battling the odds out in the typical New Zealand bush.

In my 12th year of high school, I caught the bus most days through typical windy gravel roads out to my aunties' place where she kept her horses. I had no time for boys or other extra-curricular after school activities, horses always came first. We had been blessed enough to have a 9,000-acre station on the coast in the Bay of Islands bordering onto our small family farm, where we could ride out our horses and practice overnighters, experimenting with techniques of hobbling, high lining, packing, figuring out what saddles fit and which don't, what tent works, a gun that might be easily carried horseback, and so on...

Every night we would crouch around Em's laptop with our splotchy Wi-Fi signal, and google as much as we could load about pack-saddles, trekking over month-long periods, floating (transporting horses via a covered trailer) horses long distances and cool stations to ride over in NZ. I might just point out here that my Aunty Emma and I are very similar with only 14 years between us, we have very similar dreams based around riding horses around areas that aren't often seen in NZ, and we aspire to one day ride the length of New Zealand together.

Although often we are mistaken for sisters, we agreed I am the optimistic "she'll be alright" sort of attitude, while Emma is more pessimistic, heading more towards a safety-first mind frame. So we balance each other out quite nicely and work well together when it comes to big decision making. Emma is the brains and the ultimate survival guide, always giving us 110%, and having served in the NZ Air Force as a medic, she has been in plenty of survival scenarios herself. Whereas I am more of a tag-along spontaneous adventurer, who's curiosity and mischievousness usually get the better of me.

So, in January 2017, we began preparing for our first big trek in the high country of the South Island, one of the most dangerously remote and vast areas in New Zealand. The dangers surrounding the high country are not expected from wild animals, as our scariest wildlife is possibly no worse than an angry boar/pig, but more from unexpected weather changes or natural disasters such as flash floods, earthquakes, and simply the risk many explorers find of getting themselves lost in the hills.

After finding a huge topographic map of Molesworth station: the largest station in New Zealand covering almost half a million acres at over 185,000hectares (ha), supporting roughly 10,000 head of cattle, it was settled. We marked out potential routes and trails we could take, popping back and forth over both Molesworth and St James station, a 78,000ha neighboring conservation area. During mid-2017, a third of Molesworth was baited in poisonous 1080 baits, dropped and spread via helicopter. Used for targeting possums, it also kills the majority of the other wildlife, including deer, pigs, and even birds that eat the poisoned carcasses and other nearby species.

We changed our plan to only ride among the safer two-thirds of the station, but still risked a potential danger for secondary poisoning, or if the helicopter had dropped baits outside of their targeted zone.

The plan essentially was to survive six weeks in the bush, with no communications, limited supplies, and three horses—two for riding and one as a packhorse. We were prepared to walk places the horses couldn't carry us and hoped to achieve around 100kms a week, taking rest days as we needed them. We would base in a paddock at Hamner Springs township, where our adventure would begin and end. We had only ever adventured out overnight with our horses several times before, all in the safety of our hometown riding over farms we knew like the back of our hand. But down south, if something went wrong, we had to toughen up and figure it out ourselves, there would be no vets to go running to and no more mum to call for help. This was the real deal.

Emma transformed her horse float into a step-up, swinging door with no bars inside, where our horses travel backward pretty much free-roaming the float. Statistically speaking, 8/10 cattle will naturally turn around to face backward on a stock truck, and we discovered that our horses enjoyed traveling this way much more than straight front-facing.

My big job was to get the horses fit. Bailey, Em's quarter horse mare who I mentioned previously was on the list to take, she was a dream to get into work. But her solid Clyde cross, Weka, was a different story. If you drove past us during one of our non-stop trots down the road, you would witness an un-coordinated sight of Weka clomping along in a very, as-slow-as-I-can-get-away-with trot, and me on her back squeezing my legs looking like a constipated child. We got there in the end.

On the 4th of December, 2017, we packed up our year's work and set off to go "bush" for six weeks in the gorgeous high country of the South Island, riding over Molesworth, St James, the village of Boyle, the Doubtful range and several other areas in the Marlborough District. This was the longest I had ever left my hometown of Kerikeri, Northland for, but I put on a brave face for the three-day drive, as Emma would need all the company and help to navigate, she could get.

Our itinerary for the journey stopped us in Te Awamutu at a friend's deer farm, a Wellington riding stable for the second night then onto a four-hour ferry-boat crossing the Cook Strait and into the most breathtaking picturesque valley on silver waters, guarded on either side by jagged outcrops and crumpled hills that looked to have kind eyes, welcoming us into Marlborough Sounds.

On the 6th of December, we took our steeds for an introductory trek down the main street of Hamner Springs, a stunning alpine spa village in the middle of nowhere. I had organized to borrow a riding horse there since we had no room to bring my own and was using our trusty old no-fail Weka as the packhorse. My lucky draw was a huge black Clyde x Station bred mare by the name of Meg, who was later nicknamed Megasaurus (mega-sore-arse) for obvious reasons.

Riding through Hamner Springs was like traveling back in time. The big abandoned hospital was built for mentally ill soldiers during the First World War and still stood proud. Their brick library surely hadn't been modified since either.

I am writing now with the help of a little blue pocket journal I kept, and it began the day with, "straight to the local pub on horseback, currently riding down the main street with an apple cider in hand, first thing off my bucket list—check."

Typical us.

After settling in we took off into the mountains aboard the truck to drop off four large food parcels we would collect during our journey, hiding our supplies in nearby DOC (Department of Conservation) huts, private mustering quarters, or small areas of civilization.

We didn't feel ready to leave, but I don't think we ever would have. On the 7th of December, we traveled 16 painfully slow and hot kilometers to the old St James homestead, tackling our first hill in a scorching temperature of 39.8 Degree Celsius. Normally, a horse is supposed to carry the rider up the hill. Well, after 100m of encouraging Meg up, I was off towing her already sweaty ass up and over Jack's pass. So, day one of going bush for six weeks was more of an Annie's-spontaneous-hill-workout fitness day.

We arrived at three old historic buildings, tentatively dated to the 1880s when the run was purchased by two Scottish brothers. These are the wool-shed, cookhouse (which would have been important to feed the many men employed during mustering season), and stable. Scattered about were also numerous old dog kennels for the muster's hounds. Poking around in the bush we discovered what remains of the homestead itself, which burned down in 1947. Em and I decided the woolshed looked most attractive for our night there, and we set our camping mats under the old shearing stands, amongst an old horse wagon for hauling out the wool bales, and other disintegrating shearing tools.

The morning of the 8th we agreed to be our first rest day. So after several hours of attempting to lure eels close with cheese to shoot them, we took off bareback into the late afternoon with the 22 magnum slung over Aunty

Emma's back, true cowboy style, and raced off to find some better game as we already felt meat deprived. I felt as though we were straight out of 'The Man from Snowy River," a classic Aussie western adventure film. Despite us both being a terrible shot, Emma managed to score our first hare, which is a common NZ pest, like a large rabbit. Slung over Meg's shoulder, we meandered back to the woolshed and cooked up a feast, stewing every scrap of meat we could scavenge off that hare.

On the 9th we rode 24km along the St James cycle trail to Scottie's hut, crossing our first-ever swing bridge which we later noticed was signposted "MAX 5 PERSONS AT A TIME." Whoops.

By this time, Weka followed us off the lead, and occasionally even lead the way over boardwalks and past cyclists. Her pack saddle was a simple fiberglass tree design, holding two large canvas panniers on either side of her. She looked after her panniers better than any packhorse would, carefully weaving between spikey matagouri bush while keeping one eye on her pack saddle to be sure not to scrape hard against anything.

A local cyclist pointed us in the direction of a thermal mud pool down by the river. We relaxed until we turned to wrinkly prunes. But riding back up the narrow track covered in short thick brush proved to be a bit more of a mission than we anticipated. Bailey, in her efforts to scramble up the steep trail, stepped into a large solid thorn and punctured her fetlock quite deeply. We treated it with Manuka honey and wrapped it clean but by the next morning, it had begun looking slightly infected. Bailey refused to let us jab her with an antibiotic's injection, throwing her body side to side and tossing her head as soon as Emma came close with the needle. Giving up, we started the 7km from Scottie's hut to Pool hut. Along the gorge, we pottered along for Bailey's sake, taking it easy. Possibly too easy. Weka decided that at this rate, she could eat and walk at the same time, and being a free-range horse snatched up a good few mouthful of tutu off the bank.

Tutu (also named Tutin or Coriaria Arborea) is a deadly poisonous river weed that grows in shrubs all over the river banks and is responsible for the greatest percentage of stock poisoning by plants in New Zealand. And our darling packhorse just ate it. Aunty Em seriously thought her horse was going to die, and all we could think to do was let her graze until she was full, to try and dilute the toxins down. So we pulled over only 2km into our short journey, again trying to give Bailey another jab of antibiotics and Bute—an anti-inflammatory—to no luck. Weka seemed OK at that moment, just ambling along like her usual self, and there was nothing else we could do, except pray.

Not five kilometers had passed when we were faced with an extreme option. Swim through a strong river that looked over 6ft deep or tiptoe over a 30-meter swing bridge, suspended a death's fall up above the river. The river looked to be our safest option, spreading out wider downstream, causing a shallower area. Bailey, who already struggled with river crossings on her small hooves was let free, while Emma jumped aboard the mighty Weka, perched like a bird on top of her pack saddle. Although times had been troubling that day, Emma and I managed to keep our sense of humor throughout it all, joking about how Weka truly was the star of the day.

Our horses powered into the chilling white water, moving forward as fast as they were shifting downstream. Bailey took her time to carefully navigate the ankle trapping boulders, but eventually made it over, looking rather proud of herself for accomplishing such an achievement on her own. I could catch a glimpse of the pool hut in the distance, but as we neared, something didn't look too right... it was a beehive, now home to thousands of swarming bees racing in and out of its soggy plastered walls. The tent it was. Later on, Em and I dressed into our baggy track pants and hoodies, mimicking bee-suits, wearing caps with our mosquito head nets over top, to cover our faces. Aunty Emma being a beekeeper by trade, insisted we don't let opportunities like this pass us up, so on we went into the human-sized beehive to give our shot at extracting some honey. To tell the truth, I don't remember getting much honey that day, nor do I remember our makeshift suits being very "bee proof."

On the 11th of December, I woke up early to check on the horses, semi expecting a half-dead Weka from her Tutin ingestion the day before. Well, my friend, Weka was still alive and well, emerging from the mist with a friendly nicker.

Today's plan was a simple 7km ride to a more excluded hut by the name of Jervois, nestled in a small clearing of beech trees and totaras. The hut itself offered an open fire pit with a corrugated iron chimney, two rat eaten bunk beds, and a pack of playing cards.

We hadn't even been in the bush for five days yet, but could already feel the relentlessness of this terrain, different from what we were used to at home. After letting a horse off to graze and high-lining the other two, we gathered wood and spent the rest of our night drinking hot lentil soup, playing cards, and relaxing in our rat-infested beds, reading some old books previous backpackers had left in the hut. For the first time in my life, I felt what true peace was like. Having battled through the last couple of days to finally being able to breathe without stress, I have only God to thank.

The following two days were glorious miracles. Weka was alive and well every morning, and Bailey's swollen fetlock had visibly diminished. We woke early during our short stay at Jervois hut to get out amongst the crisp morning dew. With the gun over our shoulder, we vaulted up onto Weka and Meg, Bailey leading the way for our morning hunt. When I say we "vaulted," what I mean is I took about 10 big strides back from my giant 16hh horse, then beelined straight for her shoulder in an ungainly sprint before half-heartedly flinging my body halfway over her back, shimmying and jigging myself further over as she walked away, clearly unimpressed at my skillful mounting technique. Vaulting was something Em and I improved on during those six weeks.

After a half-hour of foraging through the spiky native matagouri, Bailey's ears pricked up and her nose went straight down to the dirt as she picked up some speed. Our much less nimble Clyde crosses followed with as much twig-snapping and bush-rattling as they could have possibly managed, but Bailey kept at her nose, like a pig dog finding a scent, nose down, tail up. We clicked that she was tracking either deer or pig scent, and she did lead us to a very pig-scuffed area where we caught a fleeting glimpse of a small boar running out of our way. Maybe Bailey was more talented than she made out to be!

Although secluded Jervois was well out of the way of other cyclists or backpackers, and offered an absolute abundance of freshwater springs and sheltered meadow grass, the sandflies were beginning to irritate the horses, causing them to itch their faces raw on the manuka and kanuka branches. Em mixed up some baby oil with fipronil to help repel the little midges, but it was hard watching poor Bailey with her much finer skin begin to swell from her ears to her muzzle.

The next day we took a long loop back to pool hut, then carried on straight to Scottie's hut for the night of the 14th. As I was frying our wraps on the open fire grill, I noticed a hawk squawking and circling above the hut area. Scottie's hut had a small square paddock which we quickly patched up with our standards and tape, so we could sleep in peace knowing the horses wouldn't be escaping that night. But the hawk kept circling and I knew something wasn't quite where it should be. Later that night, a blood-curdling screech jumped at us from under a nearby bush. Emma, being the gutsier out of us led the way by torchlight, while I nervously followed as though I was in a horror movie, about to be booby-trapped and strung up in a net by native cavemen or what not… my thoughts could get out of control.

Emma gasped, "ANNIE, A KITTEN!" And to my surprise, it was.

A fluffy little tabby kitten with bright green eyes stared back at us in the torchlight, no bigger than a hedgehog. Wild cats are a huge pest in these DOC areas, killing heaps of native birds and insects, so it wasn't uncommon to find cat traps nestled around corners or in trees. This is most likely how the mother of this kitten died. There was no way we could leave the poor bugger there to be eaten by that hawk, no doubt, so we took him into the hut and mixed him up some milk powder formula, which he gulped up like, well, as any starving kitten would.

After much debate over a name, Emma let me dub him, "Scottie," since he was found at Scottie's hut. Whenever we collected our ponies ready for a bareback adventure, Scottie would pounce up behind us and follow like a true trooper, occasionally riding up on horseback when he lagged.

Later that night a cute hunter rocked up to the hut on his quad bike. He had some venison and a hare which he offered to us. We gladly accepted since our aim recently had been pathetic, we hadn't eaten meat since that first hare Em shot. Then Em asked about Scottie… the cute fella offered to shoot him for us, so we didn't have to commit to taking him along on our journey, and if we left him behind he would surely be snapped up by that hawk.

Eventually, after Em humming and hawing about keeping Scottie and me just staring googly-eyed at the first male I had seen in over a week, she sighed and told him thanks, but no thanks. He tipped his head and gave us a wink after "hooning off" (driving recklessly) into the darkness.

Scottie held our girl gang of five together like a true man. We began the journey back towards St James headquarters in case Bailey or Weka did need some medical attention. Emma cozied him up into her sheepskin saddle pad, leading him on Bailey. Every river crossing, we dunked him underwater to cool his tiny body, and after several dips, he became rather fond of the water and began getting in on his own accord for a cool-off.

One time while we were washing in the Clarence, he jumped in to follow us and got completely washed downstream before we could catch up with him! 24kms later we reached the homestead wool-shed, and much to our delight met up with some other riders heading back to town the next day, one of the older ladies adoring our little mascot. After some good banter and beers, she agreed to give him a home. I almost cried that night, snuggling up with Scottie on my chest. He was a legend, coming out to help catch the horses, helping me collect wood for our fire and he nearly caught on fire once when he got too close, letting a stray ember land on him!

The next few days we hung around the wool-shed, riding out up the ski field with the local horse group, and even found a place of reception. I called mom for the first time that day, it was so comforting to hear her voice, and remembered that we can both look up and see the same stars.

Em caught a ride to town for some emergency errands, visiting the vet about the Tutin and getting one of Bailey's shoes replaced. So yes, Tutin is deadly to ruminants like cows and sheep, but not to horses thank the Lord. Before we left Northland, we got our farrier to teach us some tips and tricks for re-nailing on a shoe. So, our skills in this department were amateur, to say the least.

19th December and we are "ON THE ROAD AGAIN" (in our best reenacting of Donkey's voice, of the movie Shrek).

By this point, we had plenty of catchphrases and movie lines that we used on the daily. As soon as we were mounted with the panniers all set to go and our horses packed up, one would exclaim in a sing-song voice, "WE'RE ON THE ROAD AGAIN, I can't wait to get on the road again…"

Then whoever played Shrek would reply in their gruffest Shrek voice, "What did I say about singing?"

Then Donkey, "Well can I whistle?"

Shrek, "No."

"Well can I hum?"

"Alright."

Then in a humming tune whoever started as Donkey would hum the "on the road again" tune.

Another oldie-goldie from the same movie is Donkeys, "ARE WE THERE YET?" Now that one, I tell you, was used on the hourly.

Today was a scorching 20kms following the Clarence River along its glacial valley to Fowler's hut, set amongst the golden tussocks at the base of the historic Fowlers Pass track. William Langley Fowler was an 1860's settler, and if you had asked the Scottish brothers what they thought of their old neighbor, they might have made some pointed comments of sheep-stealing, and locking his wife inside the small two-room hut whenever he went out. Although I was told that one day she escaped and he never saw her again.

The day after, we carried on following the Clarence river, when about 5km into our 25km journey I was hit with heat exhaustion and serious dehydration. I felt like dying. The blazing sun didn't help at all, so I held my saddle horn feeling utterly gross and uncomfortable as if I might throw up. After a scull of water and reluctantly carrying on, we found Island Gully hut, but our day hadn't finished yet.

Em caught us another hare, which we cooked up into a "beef stroganoff" stew. While we were preoccupied settling into Island Gully, we heard a faint thud of hoofbeats echoing over the hill. Our horses. I suppose they too were unsatisfied with tussock, yet again for dinner, and had wandered off to find better forage. I raced out in my underwear and bare feet to track them down.

As I reached them wandering along a rocky creek, our two following Meg's cheeky lead, I realized in my hurry I had forgotten their halters. Bailey stopped and turned back to me, Weka following her lead, but Meg and I still hadn't bonded yet and she couldn't have cared less about me. Bailey, being an easy height of 14.1hh to vault onto was picked as my alpha mare, and we rode back to the hut at complete liberty, Weka trailing behind. After we disappeared over the hill, Meg decided she better catch up as well. What a relief.

The 21st greeted us with a crisp mist hiding the jagged mountain range we would soon be crossing. Just past the Sedgemere sleepout, we spotted some lakes dotted with ducks. A good friend of Emma's used to tell her how easy it is to catch a duckling or a flapper; a large duckling almost ready to fly but not yet getting airborne, normally quite plump and fatty. He would explain, "you just chase them 'till they tire, otherwise you might find them hiding in the reeds and bushes, so if you're quiet, you could look for their tails sticking out and go in for a tackle."

If you had been a passerby that day, you would've stopped in your tracks to laugh at two girls who had stripped off into their bras and undies, running around with their hands outstretched towards the flappers they found. After finding the girls having no luck on their feet and having chased all the nearby birds into the middle of the pond, you would probably be rolling on the ground laughing as they waded waist-deep into the sludgy mud, attempting to corner the flappers between them than diving aimlessly at the paranoid birds.

I couldn't have imagined what we looked like after our swim that day, but it wouldn't have been pretty. Giving up, we crawled out of that pit shaking like dogs. As we squelched towards our clothing pile, I parted the reeds to check one last bush and what do you know, a hiding duckling! I tackled it as though I was playing in the NRFL, and leaped up presenting my catch to Em, for her to kill, of course, I wasn't that tough yet.

The 22kms to Brookdale homestead was bliss. We cantered all the flats, Weka bounding in front with her pack bouncing along with her ungainly stride. But if I thought the vast expanse of the rocky flats inhabited by a never-ending herd of black Angus cattle was beautiful, then Brookdale itself was something else. I will never be able to fully detail the feeling this place gave me, but if I were a drover back in the 1800s, this is where you would find me.

Over a crystal-clear river and through draping's of green leafy vines, we emerged into a clearing of the tidy post and rail paddocks, some boasting willow, and poplar trees, others the remains of rusty carts and horse plows. Some yards to my left, dog kennels to my right, then into what I could only describe as the Garden of Eden. A blue rocky raceway sidled by more white fencing leads us into a small village of white rammed earth buildings with trendy matching red roofs creating a very homely feeling. A woodshed, and a stable with rows of different sized horseshoes neatly stacked on the walls, next to a forge. Several rows of shearers or shepherds' quarters, all with sprung mattresses and matching bedside candles. Deer antlers stood out on the white exterior walls, it was all a cowboy fairyland. But the homestead itself possessed a huge brick fireplace, a matching dining table with brick stands, and a bold black brick kitchen area. The occasional lariat hung over a couch, helplessly left behind after the previous muster, and a longhorn skull sat above some rolling stained wood doors. Majestical.

Unfortunately, we couldn't stay here forever, so after cooking our duckling in an underground hot-rock style, we hunkered down in the stables, our horses looking right at home amongst the weeping willows. We couldn't resist at least one day to explore more of Brookdale's secrets, where I was proud to have claimed my first target, shooting, skinning, and gutting my first hare (which so happened to be blind in one eye).

On the 23rd we traveled 35kms past Segway hut, where we found a jar of raro awaiting us. The terrain got steeper as it got boggier, so we headed uphill to try and avoid the bogs—to no luck. Meg and I went down in a flash, squelching and bunny hopping around back to safety. We knew that cattle could walk through the same bogs that could also claim the lives of horses. Weka wondered what we were waiting for and navigated ahead of us, sliding carefully downhill to a dryer track across. If it wasn't for Weka that day, we might've had to turn around back to Brookdale homestead. The big bay packhorse effortlessly tried and tested different patches of ground, occasionally backing off and re-routing us on her own accord. We followed without hesitation or interrupting her.

We rode 40km on Christmas eve, after getting stuck behind a fence with no end or gate in our sight we treated ourselves to a tin of sweetened condensed milk, boiled into the caramel. Exhausted horses and exhausted riders called for a refreshingly freezing river wash.

Christmas day! We started out walking on foot to give the horses a break, but I was quick to jump aboard Meg. Bailey and Weka had picked up a pace faster than we could keep up with, like how horses always get energy heading home. There was no point trying to race after them, so Em jumped on behind Meg, and we doubled a good 10km, crossed the Clarence, and ended up near Fowler's hut again. Bailey and Weka must have remembered the hut from a week back, and we laughed as we saw them both in the distance crossing the road and being let through the hut gate by an older couple cooking pancakes. As soon as we caught up on our one loyal steed, we found ourselves seated at a makeshift log table, enjoying a hearty Christmas breakfast of pancakes with some new company.

Then onwards and upwards to Fern Gully, mysteriously marked on our map with a single square and X, so we didn't know what to expect at our next destination. Well, after 30km of pushing under chain floodgates and letting Weka guide us through more mish-mash bogs, we emerged from the bush to look down over another stunning Brookdale replica. This homestead had smaller, individual cabins, again with fully fenced paddocks for our horses. Our Christmas planned food parcel was a short 8km ride from Fern Gully to the Acheron house, and we spotted plenty of potential Christmas trees up in an overgrown yard, so it was settled. We would stay there for three nights for our rest, the horses to recover from some small saddle sores, and to celebrate Christmas.

To give Weka a break, Em and I tacked up Bailey and Meg with their empty saddlebags and began our short ride to the Acheron house, noticing some good potential fishing spots on our way, Weka happily trailing alongside us.

When we arrived at the old plastered cabin, we were greeted by a big Christmas family gathering camping nearby, similar to what our own family would be doing back home, just 1,300km away. So after packing our supplies into the saddlebags, we introduced ourselves and were invited for lunch, consisting of leftover Christmas turkey, meats, fruits, crackers, cheese, and many other foods that we had forgotten existed.

The kids were nuts over our horses, and after letting one girl sit on Bailey, we were bombarded with 10 more children calling shotgun and arguing over who will ride what horse.

After two hours of swimming with the kids and horses in the nearby river, on the boundary of the recent 1080 drop, Em and I were desperate to dig into our new supplies, so politely said our goodbyes and rode off into the sunset.

That night was the hardest day emotionally for me. It was my first Christmas without mom, so I tried to take my mind off that sad fact while sorting through our supplies: food into the food bags, propane gas, lighters, and other objects into our materials bag. But there was something extra in this supply package. A container that only mom would have thought to put together, with home-baked gingerbread men, ready-to-pipe icing, and other delicious decorations for us to decorate the cookies, cream and brandy snaps, fairy lights, treat-filled stockings for the horses, Christmas pies, peppermints, Malteser chocolates, coffee sachets, some gifts from Aunty Annalisa, but most memorably, there was a small stack of 7 letters, some addressed to Em and some to me.

Mom had gone around to close friends and family and had them write us the most heartwarming letters to open for Christmas.

With tears in my eyes, we went foraging for a decent looking pine tree, each finding a couple of saplings which we nestled together into the corner of Emma's cabin, complete with fairy lights and candy canes. There we huddled up together, decorating gingerbread, sharing memories, and reading our cards out aloud. One of my brothers wrote, "Oh, and don't worry, I am using up all your hot water in my showers." I will forever cherish that night of the 26th, sobbing and laughing together, then bringing the horse's stockings out for them to utterly demolish the contents of peppermint and baked apple treats.

The 27th brought a morning thunderstorm upon us as we stood in the

Clarence river trying our luck at trout fishing, so we packed up and rode back to our homely base at Fern Gully through the sleet and hail pounding us from every direction. The snow had already begun to settle on the distant mountain tops. From riding in mid-30-degree Celsius (86°F) temperatures two days ago to now minus zero (32°F) was a big shock for our horses. The cold was relentless on all of us shivering uncontrollably. As soon as it cleared, we were back on the horses at liberty attempting yoga and balancing tricks while we rode them around aimlessly to warm up.

On the 28th we backtracked back to Fowler's hut, a hearty 24km through some pig-infested bush tracks, where Bailey went all pig-dog style again sniffing them out. Emma has put a new command on her, to get her hyped up for pig chasing, by yelling, "GO BAILEY GO!" and letting her sprint off following whatever scent she may have picked up. So when we get bored or if Emma was calmly riding down a hill, I would find it extremely entertaining to ride up alongside her and Bailey and yell, "GO!" in Bailey's ear, where Bailey in response would gather her hindquarters under herself and excitedly boost off, snatching the reins out of Em's hands, leaving me in the dust, and in complete hysterics.

As we neared the road, we parked up on a river bed for a quick snack, looping the horse's ropes over their saddle horns for a graze. Meg still hadn't particularly bonded with me, and couldn't care less about any loyalty she might have been signed up for on this trip, so took all her chances to head home, solo.

As soon as I noticed her straying away from our group, I leaped up to bring her back, but to my surprise she started into a trot, zooming over the small boulders as if they weren't even there. I couldn't negotiate the river bed as smooth as she could, and the only thing going through my mind was the fact that the number of fences between here and her home town: was zero.

Suddenly Emma's voice echoed out to me from the other side of the river. With a beaming smile on her face, she let Bailey tear after Meg while whoop-whooping and yee-hawing. She's always been quick to act, sometimes quickly re-routing us on what she assumed was a "shortcut," which would usually turn out to be a good hour longer, but that day I was thankful for her tearing off after my runaway horse, without too many second thoughts concerning Bailey's legs or Weka getting left behind. Weka, as per usual, stayed put content with her grassy patch.

After reuniting with my "oh-so-favorite horse," we picked up some speed weaving under the giant power pylons, following old cattle tracks between the Clarence and the gravel road—the never-ending border between St James and Molesworth Station.

The sun in the middle of the day was lumbering above us, the Clarence babbled a steady rhythm, its' crystal-clear water reflecting a skewed image of the brown mountains opposite us. Gorse flowers popped in tune with the tui and cicadas. Heaven on Earth.

By this day we had spent a total of nearly 350 km in the saddle, and my wide shouldered mare with her big Clyde conformation was different compared to the smaller bush ponies my body was used to riding back home. I still get a sore bum thinking about it. This is where the nickname for my giant steed came in useful—Megasaurus. But when referring to Meg from my glute pains, you would put more emphasis on the mega-SORE-ass. So to mix it up, Em and I rode the rest of the way to Fowlers backward, cross-legged, or standing up, Weka in front navigating the cattle routes for us while we sang our hearts out to "Hakuna Matata" and other Lion King songs. Many passersby are slowed right down to photograph our amusing riding styles.

Fowler's pass is one of the more common attractions in this area, being easily accessible by the road to cyclists and trampers.

We woke early on the 29th to try and beat the scorching sun. It was a steep terrain. We walked 14km on foot, leading the horses along narrow biked-sized tracks which dipped and rose as much as any rollercoaster would. A falcon swooped over our heads, guarding her nearby nest.

After sliding down the other side of Fowlers pass we could just make out Stanley Vale hut hidden behind a couple of oaks down in the valley. The hut rested peacefully uphill from the picturesque lake Guyon, beneath snow-capped mountains growing into the distance.

This was a view I had only ever seen on postcards. Em, and I glanced at each other totally in awe of our surroundings, knowing we both wanted to stay here longer than just one night.

Good company awaited us at Stanley Vale, one who happened to be a very well-known horseman in both NZ and the USA, who we still keep in contact with and have since attended his horsemanship clinics.

The next few days consisted of bareback boosts, swimming the horses, many fishing attempts with the old hut rod, and chasing Canadian geese in the hope of another meat meal.

On the 31st, we rode a steep 13km up the mountain towering beside Lake

Guyon, for a beautiful 360-degree view of 8 deep gullies; some a vibrant yellow overtaken with broom bush, some brown and rocky, others a luscious green, all leading to different areas of St James. This was the highest altitude we have ridden yet, at 1,434m (roughly 4,700 feet).

Halfway up Lake Hill, Bailey pricked her ears towards a gaggle of Canadian geese, most of them flappers. Em couldn't sit still. Adrenaline pumped through me as we urged our horses into a gallop chasing the goslings up the hill. The group split up so we naturally chose a decent-sized flapper each, locking our horses onto our targets. Once they tired we leaped off the horses and chased our worn-out flappers, Em practically flinging herself off Bailey mid-canter and diving onto her catch. I took a bit more encouragement from Emma cheering me on from the sidelines, eventually capturing my gosling. I won't go into detail for the end part, it can only be described as "pull starting a lawnmower." Two more geese each and we made our way proudly back to Stanley Vale, plucking and stuffing the four fat birds then using the local possum trappers camp oven to slow cook over a fire.

I strung up the fairy lights from Christmas along the old wooden bunk beds, and we spent the rest of our night enjoying an old beer we found chilled in a nearby spring for New Year's Eve.

New years was celebrated with a 9 pm night ride on Weka and Bailey, cantering bareback up an extremely steep windy trail through the short bush. I lay there on Wekas back as the sun set, observing the stars and the way the moon highlighted the jagged hilltops surrounding us.

Riding down from our ridge was terrifying, with one hand knuckled down onto Wekas withers, leaning back until my head was almost touching her rump. I closed my eyes and put all my trust in this mighty beast.

Meg was asleep under the oaks when we got down at 10 pm but the moon had completely illuminated our surroundings, so again we took off downhill through open fields to Lake Guyon, photographing the evening and completely enjoying ourselves along with the bats swooping through the nearby forest.

The second day of two thousand and eighteen provided us with thunder and lightning, leaving the horses tucked up in one of the sturdiest paddocks we had been fortunate to come across.

We had brought along the tape and several fence standards for nights we couldn't high-line, but Stanley Vale was equipped with a full manuka railed paddock, total peace of mind for us knowing the horses were safe that day.

Later, we each dug a hole to help the local possum trapper erect a hitching rail.

After farewelling Stanley Vale, we carried on North/Westbound past the Ada Homestead, to the Anne hut for the night of the 3rd. The original Anne hut burned down in 2010, but because the Anne hut is directly on the Te Araroa Trail (marked trails for cyclists and trampers to walk the length of NZ, cape to bluff), it was recently rebuilt in the middle of a bush clearing to a large 20-bed cabin, maintained full-time by a hut warden.

We didn't get there nearly as quick as we had anticipated, taking one of Emma's famous "short cuts" cutting across a dried-up river bed down in a gut, rather than riding around. We came out a couple of kilometers up the wrong valley, taking us in a loop towards saddle spur—which we used to see on the other side from pool hut. Yikes. In our lost state, Weka barged past bailey, catching the 22 Magnum on Bailey's saddlebags and snapping the stock off of the gun.

After 30kms of detouring, our horses fidgety and on the verge of losing the plot, we backtrack and finally canter up to the Anne hut, swarming with tourists from all over the world. I could only make out some German and English accents. It looked almost too civilized here for us, so we carried past hoping to find the ruins of the original hut.

After wading through a slow friendly river, we stumbled onto the old concrete surrounds, offering nothing but rubble. There was, however, a fully functioning 7 wire battened horse paddock. An ice-cold skinny dip in the river helped wash the day away. We set up Em's small alpine tent for the first time this trip, and let the horses off to graze, hanging our sweaty gear up on the fence to dry.

Wishful thinking. It rained non-stop all night. I woke to Emma shaking me at 5 am, "Annie get up," she demanded, "Baileys been neighing since dawn so I got up to see if there were wild horses, after looking for a few minutes I couldn't see anything unusual. Until I noticed Meg has gone." I slipped on my boots and went out to prove her wrong. There was no way Meg could have escaped this paddock. It was the most horse proof they had been in yet with plenty of rough prairie grass, Kikuyu, and paspalum. But Em was right. We jumped on Bailey and Weka practically straight out of our sleeping bags still wearing just thermal underlay, and let Bailey take the lead sniffing out Meg's runaway route.

We came across the black mare a couple of kilometers from camp, still on her mission away from us. Cheeky horse.

With the horses all awake we pondered back to camp to tack up for a day of exploring some nearby gullies. We made it 20km out to the Christopher hut where we rode with a small herd of wild horses, the famous tough St James breed. The St James horses are mustered in biannually where they are auctioned off at top dollar for show hunter, trekkers, dressage, eventing, and more recently for polo. Caught up in the magic of riding with the herd we barely noticed the thunder lurking overhead until it was too late.

A storm was brewing and creeping up quickly behind us, sheet lightning flickering back and forwards in the sky, so on that note we pivoted our horses and galloped through the fields of barley grasses, hurdling rivers and dodging the occasional tree. Weka was loose with only her hobbles around her neck like a collar; she had built up quite an impressive stamina and strength after four weeks carrying a 70kg pack load, pounding off ahead of us, stretching out and sticking her nose up to catch the wind.

It got to a point where we could barely carry on walking under the harsh rain and hailstones, our horses practically walking backward with their heads bent down under their chests. We pulled over to shelter under a thick matagouri bush, while we both emptied our boots of water and Emma strapped her wide-brimmed hat over Bailey's ears to stop the water from getting in.

The trickling river we had skipped over this morning was now rapidly flowing from all the mini flash floods that had fed into it. Red in color and filled with dangerous branches, we couldn't justify crossing it safely, but there was no other way over. Discovery of the day: Meg CAN clear a three-meter spread and a 1.2-meter fence. I'm just glad I stuck on during her ungainly leap over the river.

We couldn't physically ride out the next day on our planned route to Magdalen Hut, as the rivers were up too dangerously high, and the trails on our map looked to be a part of the river itself.

On the 6th of January, we woke up to heaps of Maggots all stuck in our thick felt saddle blankets. Gross. After picking each little maggot off the pads, we set off on a slow journey through steep, narrow paths weaving through a forest of beech trees and climbing rocky banks over the Ann saddle.

At one point we came to a skinny, partially rotten boardwalk across some bogs. We'd had our fair share of bogs, but weren't keen on dealing with horses breaking and falling through the rotten boards either. After trying our luck further up the swampland and only getting deeper into bogs, Weka came to her senses seemingly remembering the boardwalk, and quite promptly walked right up to it and straight over with no hesitation. I suppose we all take risks in life, even horses.

The map was true to its word and had us riding the riverbed for more than half the ride, the river settled enough to wade between its ankle-breaking boulders.

More often than not we missed the small orange arrows pointing us back on track and took some rough river detours that had the horses almost swimming. 23km later we reached a hut set in the middle of a 100acre paddock.

Meg has become my little (big) star, attempting everything we threw at her with a can-do attitude. She has leaped creeks that were too difficult to walk into, slid effortlessly down almost vertical scree-slopes, kept a loping canter in times of hurry, picked her feet up carefully through rocky gorges, and taken every chance presented to her to sneak off home.

With our rifle now a pistol, we gave up targeting hares and geese. Our next food parcel awaited us at the Hillary Outdoors Centre in the small village of Boyle. Consisting of just a gas station and a quarry. The instructors at the outdoor training camp gave us blueberries and grapes. I will never take the abundance of fruit we have back home for granted ever again.

We rode 35km past the Boyle, picked up our supplies, and carried on down the main road, back and forward over the widespread river bed of the Boyle merged into the dingy, rough gut of the Doubtful river. Weka was a pro at shuffling her butt over between two trees, glancing behind to her pack load making sure it would safely fit between both obstacles, then continuing once she was happy with the gap.

After a good hour or two of a rough track clearing with fallen trees, we passed the doubtful river hut, no more than a tin shack with barely any room for our horses to sleep. But further up onto the grassy river flats we stumbled across the Doubtless hut; a 6 bunk DOC hut with a small paddock of beech trees for our horses to enjoy. When we left Northland, our horse's diets had consisted of well-grazed stock pasture with rough grass-like Kikuyu and paspalum, clovers if they were lucky. They never ate many bush and tree leaves, but down here they can't get enough of the beech trees. It surprised me how well they have adapted their diet to suit these rough southern landscapes.

After talking myself into stripping off for a much-needed wash, I concluded that it was so unbelievably freezing because the whole river was essentially just melted snow. The source of the Doubtful river began in the Doubtless Ranges just 10km upstream at the top of the Southern Alps, one of New Zealand's most well-known attractions and largest mountain range, where you will find NZ's highest peak on Mt Cook.

While I was pre-occupied numbing my body from head to toe, Emma tramped up Amuri pass, looking over steep jungle towards the west coast, which blended into tussocky valleys with huge snow-capped mountains in the East as far as the eye could see.

We carried out almost eight kilos of booze trash from that hut, wrapped tightly on top of Weka's pack saddle, and dropped it off at the Boyle.

Then 35km back to Magdalen hut to get a good night's rest for what would unknowingly be our most challenging part of the trek.

We woke at 6 am on the 10th of January, 2018, aware we would have a big day trekking through unseen land. As I hauled Meg's big Fort Worth Texas western saddle onto her back along with her four saddlebags and tightened her girth, I noticed her girth holes had gone up three on the front and four on the back! We said our farewells to Magdalen hut at 7:30, headed east along the border of Glenhope Station.

Our day began as a mission just riding through simple flat farmland, having to work our way through run-down fence-lines pulling out old gates, or occasionally cutting tangled wires. Past Steyning hut then bypassing a locked gate via the river, which took even more bush bashing to get through. After riding through the misty haze over a saddle, it all went downhill from there, literally and figuratively.

We came off Glenhope station thinking we could follow the marked route on our map, but as we aimlessly bush bashed our way through 'The Narrows," a thick maze of broom and matagouri that bashed us more, we should have re-evaluated our situation then. The dead goose hung by its neck in a broom tree was another sign for us to turn back. But together having accomplished five weeks of hearty riding through the toughest terrain of our lives, Em and I were not about to turn around now. We rode to the edge of the Waiau River, an extremely rapid flowing river that I wouldn't even raft down. Somebody that we had passed earlier must have told us about a four-wheel drive track over the other side of the river, so we pressed on and slowly but steadily rode through the Waiau.

Making slow progress in the pouring rain assuming our challenge of the day had just been overcome was short-lived. Only moments later Bailey threw a shoe. Emma searched out our farrier tools from the pannier and began to re-nail on a spare front shoe we had brought. When Emma has something that needs getting done, she is always the girl you can trust who won't stop until it is 100% completed. But our first attempt of re-nailing a shoe in the slippery rain, with numb fingers and impatient horses, proved harder and harder as she gave it a second, third and fourth try.

18 nails and a thermos of hot pasta later, we slowly encouraged on our grumpy and struggling horses further upstream. I walked up a giant scree slope to see if I could find our bearings, but it was clear that we were lost. It got to a point where we could no longer safely step over the boulders in the shallow water, nor could we fit through the thick scrub up on the bank. One ungainly rock rolled down off the bank smashing onto Bailey's leg, trapping her hoof in between two rocks for a short period.

I could tell Emma was getting worried, both of us struggling to walk on foot ourselves, me leading Meg. Bailey was sick of boulder bashing, and her fine legs weren't doing her much help so on that note she turned around and re-crossed over the Waiau river before we could stop her, the water over her chest height. Our horses turned to follow the alpha mare's lead, so Emma, currently without her riding horse leaped on top of Weka, crouching over the bars of her pack saddle as she let her horse carry her to the other side. Meg followed suit. But just 50 meters further upstream we ran into a dead end. So now we were back to square one so it felt.

It took a heap of encouragement to get those three mares back over the river, this time almost swimming through the current. We arrived on the shore of a long bush covered hill. The only way out of our situation was up. We had been battling the Waiau river for almost three hours now and we're glad to set foot on normal land again. It wasn't a normal hill though. The Manuka was so thick we had to hand saw almost 50 trees down, meanwhile dragging our reluctant horses up the slippery hill. It was so vertical that we kept bigger distances between the horses, incase one lost her footing and slipped back down.

Spotting a deer clearing, we followed the deer tracks which looped around and around in pointless circles, I have no idea how even the deer can get out of them! But out of the corner of my eye, I spotted the faint markings of tire tracks in the distance. And it was! Emma and I skipped and danced down that four-wheel drive track like Alice in Wonderland. The track led directly onto the Cycle trail which we followed back to Scottie's hut. It was extremely confusing how we had ended up where we did, but instead of carrying on in the dark to our planned campsite, we settled down in the comfort of Scottie's hut again.

That day was the most mentally challenging and energy-draining for not just us but the horses as well. It was extremely hard on their feet, our own feet were also aching and wrinkly from wet boots. The horses each got a bowl of warm lentils that night, especially Weka for giving us 101% with her bravery, courage, and reliable attitude today. She always gives her all and keeps going even when she's exhausted and the going gets tough. I suppose she's motivated to get a feed and sleep just like us. I'm pretty sure I had athlete's foot after all that. I was thankful. We could have come out a whole lot worse than just a foot infection.

The 11th was deserving of sleep in, then dragged our reluctant steeds out into the drizzle only to climb up to an altitude of 1,000m, literally riding through the clouds. Emma had found a short cut to Stanley Vale, which we took without questioning. If any of her shortcuts were going to work, then I prayed today would be the day. It was majestical riding through the wildflowers and mosses, all faded behind the fog.

The Maori name for New Zealand is Aotearoa, meaning "land of the long white cloud." Now I knew what that really meant. Meg walked out beneath me, her ears pricked and curious, interested as I was to see what was through the clouds. Weka stuck close by so she didn't lose us.

And who would've guessed that just 20kms later, we bounded up behind the comforting sight of Stanley Vale, smoke already billowing out from its chimney?

A big pinto horse whinnied out to our mares from out on the open flats. The old possum hunter who we had met earlier must still be here. His horse was called "No-Name," and free roamed around the hut without restraints.

"He won't be expecting us yet," I told Em as we rode up.

"We told him we would be 8-10 days from when we last left," Em replied.

"Yeah well, it's only been three," I said matter-of-factly. It had been nine days.

All my undies were wet, so I went to bed with wet underwear that night but other than that, our horses were stocked with a handsome gelding to chat up for new company, and Em and I were happy having some human company from the possum trapper and his daughter.

Our next few days at Stanley Vale was a holiday in our holiday, we almost moved in permanently!

Emma finally caught a trout from Lake Guyon, and we spent most of our rest days swimming and reading all the books left in the hut. I got through the complete originals of "Alice in Wonderland" and "Alice through the looking glass."

But after separating the lentils from the split peas from the barley in our soup mix, we decided we needed an adventure for the following day, tagged along with the possum trapper on No-name, and his daughter riding Weka.

On the 14th we tacked up our horses leaving all Weka's pack gear behind in the hut. I used Emma's sheepskin saddle cover as a bareback pad, held onto Meg by a surcingle. 18km up a gorgeous valley guarded on either side by scree slopes and rocky ledges, some boasting a silver layer of snow along its ridge. The new Waiau hut was swarming with Te Araroa trail walkers.

Before I knew it, Em and I were off swimming in more melted snow with some American skinny dippers. It was an oasis up here, blissfully peaceful, with hot rocks to warm upon.

The following day, the possum hunter led the way up Maling pass, overlooking another stunning flat lake. We climbed from Maling pass (1300m) to 1600m in just eight minutes! Riding Meg bareback I found myself practically laying parallel to her own body with my arms tight around her neck as she hauled the both of us diagonally up the shale slope, held lightly together with prairie grasses and spinifex grass. We eventually hit the 1800-meter alt mark on our map, walking through vibrant greenery of flaxes and small fairy ponds. Emma walked behind Bailey holding her tail so her steed could haul her up the hills we walked on foot. Clever. Our horses had become so tolerant of us throwing whatever we had to at them, taking it all in their stride. It had been 26km of ridge riding today. Spectacular.

On the 16th we had planned a three-part ride back to Hamner Springs over three days. But after we set off briskly over Fowler's pass, we decided to trot the road back to the Woolshed. The horses were in bright spirits, Weka hooning in front, trotting like nobody could stop her. Em had stashed two ciders in the dog kennels at the Homestead, so after a drink, we decided to run the third part of our journey home all in the same day. The horses all elegantly cantered across fields following their noses home. We even arrived down at Hamner springs in time for ice cream. We deserved it after that hot 48km ride!

The locals barely recognized Meg with her lighter coat and tucked up belly, we all must've looked like cavemen as we rode through Hamner that day. Over 700 kilometers later.

I had never challenged myself so mentally and physically before. It wasn't just a few struggles we came across on our journey, it was the whole journey in itself that together Em and I overcame. Of course, we couldn't have done it without our three superstar mares. I'm now aware of what Em and I are capable of as a team, we do balance each other out, encouraging the other one on and sharing the stress when problems arise. I will be forever grateful to have had this opportunity.

*We have since received emails about our mascot Scottie, telling us that they found him out in the paddock on top of the lady's mini pony one day, and described him as a very unusual cat, enjoying both a swim in the stream and playing in the sprinkler. Miss you boy.